Practicing
Evaluation

To John, Jeni, TJ, and Libby, who make everything possible

Practicing
Evaluation
A Collaborative Approach

Rita G. O'Sullivan
University of North Carolina

SAGE Publications
International Educational and Professional Publisher
Thousand Oaks ▪ London ▪ New Delhi

For information:

Sage Publications, Inc.
2455 Teller Road
Thousand Oaks, California 91320
E-mail: order@sagepub.com

Sage Publications Ltd.
1 Oliver's Yard
55 City Road
London EC1Y 1SP
United Kingdom

Sage Publications India Pvt. Ltd.
B-42, Panchsheel Enclave
Post Box 4109
New Delhi 110 017 India

Printed in the United States of America

Library of Congress Cataloging-in-Publication Data

O'Sullivan, Rita G.
Practicing evaluation : a collaborative approach / by Rita G. O'Sullivan.
      p. cm.
Includes bibliographical references and index.
ISBN 0-7619-2545-7 (Cloth) — ISBN 0-7619-2546-5 (Paper)
    1. Participatory monitoring and evaluation (Project management)
2. Evaluation research (Social action programs) I. Title.
HD69.P75O86 2004
361′.0068′4—dc22

                                    2003017870

Printed on acid-free paper.

04   05   06   07   08   09   10   9   8   7   6   5   4   3   2   1

Acquiring Editor:	Lisa Cuevas Shaw
Editorial Assistant:	Margo Crouppen
Production Editor:	Claudia A. Hoffman
Copy Editor:	Catherine M. Chilton
Typesetter:	C&M Digitals (P) Ltd.
Indexer:	Molly Hall

Contents

Preface

This book reflects 20 years of my evaluation practice across a variety of places and programs. From those experiences, I have synthesized an approach called *collaborative evaluation*. I have learned and continue to learn by doing. Through working with clients, consulting sources, and reflecting on my practice with colleagues, I have taken tried-and-true, clearly marked evaluation paths. I also have explored some new ways to trek through less mapped territory to make sense of program evaluation.

A compelling desire to contribute to the progress of social service programs has sustained my efforts in evaluation. For me, the purpose of evaluation is to help programs understand the effects of their actions. I believe that people who work in programs are most likely to improve them after they see their current levels of accomplishment. Collaborative evaluation engages them in the evaluation process and moves them forward to this goal.

At heart, I am a pragmatist, solving problems by designing evaluations that meet clients' needs. On occasion, evaluation challenges have emerged that forced me to find solutions by creating novel methods. From the sum of my pragmatism has emerged the theoretical approach of collaborative evaluation that generalizes my experience. I believe it may be useful to others interested in similar activities.

The book has a number of intended users. For experienced evaluators, I hope that this book contains some novel variations within the realm of collaborative, participatory, and empowerment evaluation that will cause them to reflect on their practice and the reasons they proceed in the manner they do. I also suspect that some of the collaborative practices described in the book will attract their attention and interest them sufficiently to attempt them. For emerging evaluators, I believe that the information in the text will be very helpful, as it includes an overview of the entire evaluation endeavor, and, though certainly shaded by the collaborative evaluation perspective, the evaluation practices described in this book are not extraordinarily different from more general types of evaluation practice. I believe this book will be extremely helpful for program personnel new to evaluation, particularly for those who have assumed evaluation responsibilities without much formal training in the field. I expect that what is presented will provide them with a more formal picture of the process, as well as with some realistic examples of what needs to occur. Finally, I believe this book will be exceptionally useful to those program personnel who must engage and work with evaluators and who want to expand their understanding of what evaluation is and how it can help them improve their programs.

I strongly believe that evaluators who follow the collaborative evaluation approach described in this book will reduce the barriers they encounter to evaluation, improve communication and cooperation with clients, and ultimately increase the usefulness of their evaluation findings.

Acknowledgments

The development of the collaborative evaluation approach has not been an isolated process. Along the way, I have been supported and inspired by any number of colleagues and their work. Throughout my career, Bob Stake and his contributions to the evaluation field have informed and sustained me. The work of other evaluators, including Jim Sanders, Blaine Worthen, Jim Altschuld, and Michael Scriven, have provided contrast and depth to my understanding of evaluation. As I gravitated toward collaborative, participatory, and empowerment evaluation, the works of Brad Cousins, Michael Patton, David Fetterman, and Abe Wandersman have enriched my thinking and practice.

I also have benefited from working with colleagues to conduct evaluations, and I owe a special note of thanks to the current staff at Evaluation, Assessment, and Policy Connections (EvAP) at the University of North Carolina at Chapel Hill who work with me daily: Muhsin Orsini, Joelle Skaga, Bonnie Dahlke, Tracy Shaw, Sharyn Levine, Shannon Patrick, Dorene Mackinnon, Miriam Chernow, Michelle Jay, Katie Taylor, and Kellie Belton. The graduate students in my classes and the participants in my evaluation training workshops have further expanded my evaluation understanding; sometimes, as with Astrid Hendricks Smith, Martha Hudson, Mary Penta, Robert Johnson, David Wyrick, and Alexey Kuzmin, those initial contacts have extended and have substantively contributed to my evaluation understanding. This book was measurably improved by David Fetterman, Douglas Young, Paul Brandon, Jean King, Hallie Preskill, and Tom Cook, who reviewed earlier manuscript drafts.

Throughout my career, my husband John O'Sullivan has been a collaborator and supporter. His evaluation perspective has greatly enriched mine. Many of the evaluation strategies presented in this book were conceived, implemented, and refined with his counsel.

Finally, the contributions of the programs that have invited me to work with them conducting evaluations must be acknowledged. Our collaborations have led to the evaluation approach presented here. I thank them for their wisdom, their dedication, and their desire to improve the programs that they implement.

1

Evaluation Practice

An Introduction

P rogram evaluation seeks answers to questions about programs that interest program staff, participants, funders, and the public. The belief undergirding this book is that almost all programs can benefit from evaluation. Further, this book presents program evaluation through the lens of a collaborative approach, arguing that the approach offers a powerful alternative that can be applied to advantage in most evaluation situations. To understand this argument, a reader first needs to understand the larger evaluation context and the author's odyssey in developing the approach.

Modern program evaluation dates from the early 1960s and has been marked by history, structured by its visionaries, and circumscribed by professional and ethical standards. In addition, the range of evaluation practice has often mirrored the personalities of evaluators and their accompanying preferences for making sense of the world, which in turn influences how they conduct evaluations and practice their evaluation arts.

This chapter briefly reviews the current evaluation context by providing an overview of evaluation practice that includes reviewing common evaluation activities and purposes, tracing the historical evolution of program evaluation, identifying common evaluation approaches, suggesting how individual preferences and styles influence evaluation practice, and presenting current professional ethical standards.

Although it is not a substitute for more comprehensive introductory evaluation texts (see, for example, Rossi, Freeman, & Lipsey, 1999; Worthen, Sanders, & Fitzpatrick, 1997), a brief review of the broader evaluation context will promote an understanding of common terminology used in the discussion of practice.

Finally, this chapter concludes with the odyssey of the author's evaluation practice, which led to the development of the collaborative approach described in the remainder of this book. It is included to particularize collaborative evaluation as evolving over a personal 20-year context. Some evaluators are more comfortable with and claim an objective reality without personality quirks, emotional motivations, or individual idiosyncrasies. The author makes no such claims. In fact, such involvement appears unavoidable and so needs to be shared to allow readers the information necessary for judging the full merit of the collaborative evaluation approach.

Activities and Purposes Common to Evaluation

Just as programs cover a broad array of activities, their evaluation purposes follow accordingly. Evaluations can measure process, products, needs, inputs, and outcomes (both intended and not). Program evaluations thus often vary with what is to be evaluated, by whom, and how. When evaluators and program staff work collaboratively, it increases the likelihood of understanding program dynamics, identifying important questions, designing feasible evaluations, gathering quality information, and interpreting the information gathered.

Evaluation provides a systematic way in which to answer questions about a program. Those questions can occur at any point during a program's lifetime or even beyond and can frame almost any aspect of the program that is of interest. Usually program sponsors, developers, or managers commission an evaluation for a specific purpose. The program context also influences how the evaluation will be conducted, and in many cases that context can be emotionally or politically charged. Evaluators therefore must understand what is to be evaluated, along with the intended purpose(s) of the evaluation and the context of the program and how they might affect the evaluation.

EVALUATION ACTIVITIES DURING THE LIFE OF A PROGRAM

Evaluation activities can occur at any juncture in the life of a program. Evaluation could begin at the point of program conceptualization, program planning, program implementation, or program completion. Table 1.1 provides some examples of evaluation activities that might occur during the life of a program. Evaluation can prove very useful even as the program is conceptualized. Evaluation activities at this point might include conducting a needs assessment or searching the literature to unearth what is already known about similar programs that have been previously implemented. Once the program is designed and funds secured, then evaluation can be very useful at the program planning stage. At this juncture, evaluation activities can focus on determining

Table 1.1   Possible Evaluation Activities During the Life of a Program

Program Conceptualization	Program Planning	Program Implementation	Program Completion
Reviewing relevant literature	Creating personnel projections	Monitoring program activities	Assessing long-term impact
Assessing needs	Establishing timelines	Developing databases	Determining program strengths
Conducting focus groups	Estimating costs	Assessing program functioning	Identifying areas for subsequent improvement
Analyzing cost effectiveness	Identifying procurement alternatives	Determining short-term impact	Assessing cost effectiveness

timelines for implementation or researching procurement options. Once the program has begun, evaluation might include establishing a system by which to monitor program activities (outputs) or developing a database to collect information that will be useful for program monitoring and short-term impact assessment. At this stage, annual reporting of program accomplishments also could be established. Finally, on completion of the program, the evaluation might assess the program's long-term impact or identify areas that future programs might improve.

POSSIBLE EVALUATION PURPOSES

Just as the life cycle of a program will influence the type of evaluation conducted, the intended purpose(s) of the evaluation also will be an essential guiding factor. Reasons for conducting evaluations vary almost as much as the programs themselves. A primary reason most programs need evaluation is to determine how they can improve. (In evaluation parlance, this is referred to as "formative evaluation," and it is contrasted with "summative evaluation," which focuses on program impact at the conclusion of a program.) In truth, although this is changing, probably the most common reason that programs currently conduct or commission evaluations is that their funding sources require it. In addition to the two purposes already identified, common evaluation purposes include assessing program impact, identifying a program's strengths and weaknesses, justifying requests for additional resources, garnering support for a particular program approach, clarifying the next phase of a project, disseminating program findings, responding to attacks on a program, and leveraging additional resources. Sometimes the evaluation purposes may be unclear, or masked, in which case evaluators must discover the actual purposes. Evaluators need to understand the purposes of the evaluation prior to designing what needs to be done for the evaluation.

UNDERSTANDING THE EVALUATION CONTEXT

The scope and breath of a program greatly influences the evaluation design. For example, a program serving 30 students in one community will require different evaluation strategies than a program serving 3,000 students in 30 communities. Similarly, an intensive treatment program that provides 400 contact hours to individuals will provide different evaluation challenges than one that provides 4 contact hours.

In addition to understanding the scope and breath of a program, evaluators also must familiarize themselves with program content. Family support programs differ from health programs, which differ from education programs. Evaluators must understand program content sufficiently to grasp how best to orient the evaluation.

Finally, each program has unique history and circumstances that could be important to the evaluation. Programs with years of history must be considered differently from those just beginning. Changes in leadership or funding sources can also greatly influence program dynamics. Evaluators must orient themselves to program characteristics and dynamics and factor them in to the evaluation.

Evaluation Research Versus Basic Research

Program evaluation is research, but it is a specialized form of research. Lack of appreciation of this distinction can mislead researchers into inappropriately imposing basic research strategies to meet situations in need of evaluation research approaches. Within the social and applied sciences, most research is considered basic in that it focuses on generalizing findings to promote understanding of a phenomenon. For example, educational psychologists study student motivation among adolescents; sociologists examine the influence of family economic status on career choices; early childhood educators study the effect of environment on subsequent achievement. Evaluation research, on the other hand, focuses on the effectiveness of a particular program at a particular place in a particular time frame. Although it is possible, generalizability of findings is usually not a primary focus. Thus evaluators research specific program effects to understand the program being evaluated, not to generalize back to some theoretical construct of the program that may be of interest to other researchers.

Another key difference between evaluation research and basic research is that evaluators work for clients who commission the evaluation; their work is guided by a contract. Basic researchers work for themselves and their peer community to add to the existing body of knowledge; when funded, their research is supported via grants. Evaluators are agents of their clients, and thus their access to data is comparable to the client's access. For example, an evaluator studying the effects of a school district's mentoring program for low-achieving middle school students will, as an agent of the school district, have access to student records that may be needed to answer evaluation questions. The school district is obligated to evaluate its program, and the evaluator, as the district's agent, acts on behalf of the district. A basic research project that needed the same information would require special permission from parents to access the data. In support of this distinction, program evaluation activities are not included as research regulated under federal guidelines protecting human subjects; for institutional review board purposes, program evaluation studies are not considered research. On the other hand, evaluators who intend to turn their evaluation data into a research study for publication do need to submit to human subjects review. This distinction, between evaluation research and basic research, should caution those who fail to recognize substantive differences in the two research approaches before they misapply a basic research paradigm to an evaluation research setting.

The Historical Evolution of Program Evaluation

Modern program evaluation was launched by Ralph Tyler (1949) in the 1930s, stimulated by categorical federal program funding in the 1960s, and refined in the 1990s through a wave of accountability and reform. Some have tried to impose theoretical frameworks onto evaluation (see, for example, Christie, 2003, for a thoughtful review of the current state of evaluation theory and practice), but at this point in the evolution of the evaluation field, a historical presentation seems more economical, in the sense that a historical treatment explains more within the limited space available. Reviewing key events in the history of modern program evaluation can assist greatly in understanding the current status of the profession.

In the 1930s, Ralph Tyler led a team that began an 8-year study to assess educational quality in the United States. He found that much of what people professed as educational goals were vague and distinctly unmeasurable. The resulting birth of the behavioral objectives evaluation movement in the United States monopolized the program evaluation field until the early 1960s.

In 1957, when the U.S.S.R. successfully launched Sputnik, the first satellite in space, the United States responded by investing sizable amounts of federal funds into educational reform; at the same time, funds were also allocated to domestic and international social programs. As early as 1963, Cronbach challenged the evaluation community, pointing out that its current level of practice was inadequate to meet the needs of the newly developed, federally sponsored curriculum reform programs. Passage of the Economic Opportunity Program in 1964 and the Elementary and Secondary Education Act in 1965 created additional programs in need of evaluation. This accelerating demand for evaluation generated interest among social science and applied researchers and led them to develop new evaluation approaches and establish university-based evaluation centers.

During the 1970s and 1980s, evaluation grew as a field and settled into its modern role. Informal gatherings of professionals who considered themselves evaluators were followed by the creation of more formal evaluation professional organizations. The first program evaluation professional standards were published in 1981. In 1985, the American Evaluation Association emerged from the consolidation of the Evaluation Research Society and the Evaluation Network.

Evaluation as a field was maturing, but the 1980s saw a shift in the demand for evaluation as federal government funding to educational and social programs declined. The dwindling resources positively affected evaluation in that sponsors became more demanding about requiring funded programs to demonstrate results. Ostensibly the lack of evaluation support was a difficult time for evaluators, but the competition for funding promoted increased appreciation of evaluation among program developers and implementers.

The decline in demand for evaluation ended in the 1990s with new federally supported curriculum reform movements and was spurred on by a booming economy that funded more social programs. These efforts were tempered by the newly acquired appreciation for accountability that began in the previous decade and thereby also increased the demand for evaluation. By the beginning of the 21st century, program evaluation emerged as an acknowledged field with established professional organizations around the globe, was guided by professional standards, and could claim a 35-year legacy of practice.

Common Evaluation Approaches

A variety of program evaluation approaches are available for evaluators' use. These approaches vary in how they embrace the evaluation task and in the audience they consider as interested in the evaluation findings. Tyler's (1949) behavioral objectives approach to evaluating programs remains the most commonly known and used approach to evaluation. Other approaches developed during the first 10 years of the modern evaluation era complement the objectives approach by allowing more aspects of a program to be evaluated.

Table 1.2   Evaluation Approaches

Approach	Primary Audiences
Objectives: Focuses on objectives to determine degree of attainment	Program sponsors, managers
Management: Focuses on information to assist program decision makers	Program managers, staff
Consumer: Looks at programs and products to determine relative worth	Public, program sponsors
Expertise: Establishes peer and professional judgments of quality	Peer group, public
Adversary: Examines programs from pro and con perspectives	Program sponsors, public
Participant: Addresses stakeholders' needs for information	Participants, staff, community members

One approach that has been gaining ground since the 1980s emphasizes the importance of including the views of program participants and other stakeholders in the evaluation process.

Worthen et al. (1997) separate evaluation approaches into six categories: objectives, management, consumer, expertise, adversary, and participant. As seen in Table 1.2, each of the six approaches has a different orientation and varies in terms of the intended audience. Although there is some overlap, the approaches define the frames of reference for an evaluation.

The objectives approach to evaluation determines the extent to which the program has achieved its intended outcomes. Sometimes evaluators must work with clients to establish or clarify the program's objectives before the evaluation can be designed and implemented. Usually the objectives approach can yield important information about a program's effectiveness, but unfortunately the emphasis on outcomes may preclude the collection of information about the programmatic aspects that contributed to meeting or not meeting the program's objectives.

The management approach considers the various aspects of programs from the perspective of those who design and administer them. One of the most commonly cited management approaches was developed by Stufflebeam (2000) to address the weaknesses of exclusively objectives oriented evaluation approaches. His model, *context, input, process, product*, provides evaluation strategies for assessing program needs (context), determining what will need to be in place to begin a program (input), monitoring the program as it unfolds to improve its functioning (process), and measuring the impact of the program (product). The management approach added more dimensions to evaluation that allowed for the assessment of program aspects beyond the attainment of program objectives.

This approach, however, was limited in that it did not directly include participants or the public as potential audiences for the evaluation.

The consumer approach takes a stance similar to *Consumer Reports* and tries to compare program alternatives to one another. Scriven (1974, 1991) has been among the strongest proponents of this evaluation stance and has suggested an evaluation checklist that program adopters should use in considering their choices. Cost-effective analyses of program options would be included in this approach, as well as meta-analyses comparing program outcomes across different program strategies.

The expertise approach directs programs to seek out peers and other experts in the appropriate field to determine the effectiveness of their programs. Accreditation and licensure activities fit this description, as they establish standards of acceptable practice and then determine which programs or individuals meet these standards. Eisner (1983; 1991) promotes another aspect of this approach with something he refers to as "connoisseurship." In this evaluation approach, an expert (sometimes cast in a role similar to that of an art critic) is invited to a program to review it and share a critique of its merits; an expert review panel would serve a similar function. Informally, the expertise approach is a very commonly used evaluation strategy: Program implementers consult with peers, whose opinion they respect, to solve problems or understand program events.

The adversary approach promotes a method of scrutiny of programs that borrows from judicial and other legal practices in the United States. In modern evaluation's early boom years, between 1965 and 1975 (when funds for evaluation flowed freely), programs were put on trial. In these instances, defense and prosecution counsels selected juries, called witnesses, and heard verdicts of program worth. More recently, these trials have been discontinued, but the approach does prove useful in circumstances wherein programs or stakeholders can benefit from presenting their "case." For example, public hearings that determine which programs should receive funding can use this approach to make decisions. Similarly, disputes within programs can be arbitrated by impartial judges. Although it is not among the most common evaluation approaches, the adversary approach can prove useful in some circumstances.

The participant approach emphasizes the importance of conducting evaluation that includes essential stakeholders. This approach has recently gained ground as a dynamic evaluation framework. Begun by Stake (1967) and supported by Guba and Lincoln (1981), evaluation approaches that are concerned with stakeholders have advanced and grown greatly since 1994. The underlying assumption of this approach is that people engaged in a program should be considered in its evaluation. Some proponents believe that evaluators should lead this participation (Cousins & Earl, 1995; O'Sullivan & O'Sullivan, 1998);

others support the notion of participant-led evaluations (Fetterman, 2001; Patton, 2002). A key advantage of the participant approach is that it includes participants' perspectives in the evaluation process.

The differences in these evaluation approaches partially reflect the tensions between quantitative and qualitative research methodologists, which permeate all of the social sciences. Early in the modern evaluation era, quantitative approaches, as espoused by Campbell and Stanley (1966), predominated. Over time, led by Eisner (1983), Stake (1978), Patton (1990), Lincoln and Guba (1985), and Fetterman (1994), qualitative approaches gained ground. Today most evaluators would recognize the importance of quality inquiry (Yin, 1994) independent of the methodological paradigm used.

Often, programs require multiple evaluation approaches. Mixing and matching evaluation approaches to meet evaluation needs is a sign of thoughtful evaluation practice. A program's evaluation needs should drive selection of the evaluation approach; the approach should not determine the choice of evaluation method. Thus experienced evaluators consider the various approaches and their applicability as they design evaluations.

Individual Preferences and Evaluation Practice

Beyond program scope and evaluation purpose, historical context, and availability of common evaluation approaches, an evaluator's practice is influenced by personal talents, values, and preferences. Applying Gardner's (1983, 1999) multiple intelligences model to program evaluation would suggest that an evaluator with great interpersonal intelligence might become expert at interviewing participants or conducting focus groups; an evaluator with very little talent in this area would be challenged to do so. Similarly, cognitive style might influence evaluation choices.

A recent study (O'Sullivan et al., 2002) tied research interest to cognitive style preference. Preference for evaluation approaches could similarly be affected. Gregorc's (1999) *Style Indicator* posits four dimensions of cognitive style: concrete sequential, abstract sequential, abstract random, and concrete random. In Figure 1.1, the map depicts the four different cognitive styles by direction. "Norths" (evaluators preferring a concrete sequential style) like order and detail; easts (abstract sequentials) prefer to start with theory. Both of these groups learn in a linear fashion. Wests (concrete randoms) prefer to accomplish tasks and are motivated by relevance. Souths (abstract randoms) are concerned about others and their feelings. Wests and souths are more holistic, global learners. More than likely, the structured evaluation approaches (objectives, management, and consumer) appeal to norths and easts, whereas wests and souths are more attracted by the less structured approaches.

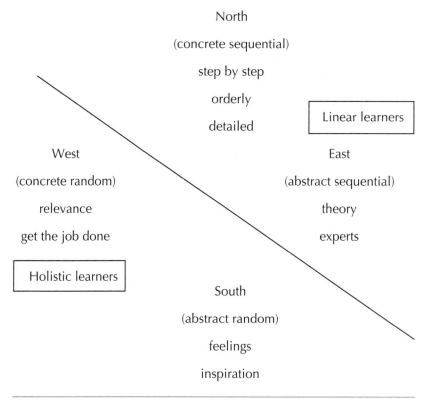

Figure 1.1   Gregorc Cognitive Style Map

As evaluation purposes should dictate evaluation design, recognizing personal preferences enables evaluators to accept or decline work that is consistent with their interests and talents.

Current Professional Ethical Standards

As in most professions, the field of evaluation is self-regulated by guidelines that set the standards for ethical practice. In the United States, the two most widely cited sources that govern quality evaluation practice are the American Evaluation Association's (AEA) *Guidelines for Professional Practice* (1995) and the *Joint Committee Standards for Educational Program Evaluation* (1994). The AEA guiding principles are excerpted here and basically identify five primary areas of concern.

- Systematic inquiry: Evaluators conduct systematic, data-based inquiries about whatever is being evaluated.
- Competence: Evaluators provide competent performance to stakeholders.
- Integrity and honesty: Evaluators ensure the honesty and integrity of the entire evaluation process.
- Respect for people: Evaluators respect the security, dignity, and self-worth of respondents, program participants, clients, and other stakeholders with whom they interact.
- Responsibilities for general and public welfare: Evaluators articulate and take into account the diversity of interests and values that may be related to the general and public welfare.

The Joint Committee standards are much more detailed but basically encompass similar areas of ethical practice.

These guidelines were developed so that everyone involved in an evaluation could be clear on the expectations. The guidelines clearly identify key elements of ethical evaluation practice. They include areas of general concern similar to those of other social science research activities, such as adherence to the protection of human subjects' rights, use of valid and reliable research methods, and concern about the potential for researcher bias or conflict of interest. Less common ethical considerations are evaluators' responsibilities to groups that have a stake in the program outcomes (e.g., the public, program staff, participants) and their obligation to provide timely and cost-effective work.

Guiding Principles for Evaluators

A. Systematic Inquiry: Evaluators conduct systematic, data-based inquiries about whatever is being evaluated.
   1. Evaluators should adhere to the highest appropriate technical standards in conducting their work, whether that work is quantitative or qualitative in nature, so as to increase the accuracy and credibility of the evaluative information they produce.
   2. Evaluators should explore with the client the shortcomings and strengths both of the various evaluation questions it might be productive to ask, and the various approaches that might be used for answering those questions.
   3. When presenting their work, evaluators should communicate their methods and approaches accurately and in sufficient detail to allow others to understand, interpret, and critique their work. They should make clear the limitations of an evaluation and its results. Evaluators should discuss in a contextually appropriate

way those values, assumptions, theories, methods, results, and analyses that significantly affect the interpretation of the evaluative findings. These statements apply to all aspects of the evaluation, from its initial conceptualization to the eventual use of findings.

B. Competence: Evaluators provide competent performance to stakeholders.
1. Evaluators should possess (or, here and elsewhere as appropriate, ensure that the evaluation team possesses) the education, abilities, skills and experience appropriate to undertake the tasks proposed in the evaluation.
2. Evaluators should practice within the limits of their professional training and competence, and should decline to conduct evaluations that fall substantially outside those limits. When declining the commission or request is not feasible or appropriate, evaluators should make clear any significant limitations on the evaluation that might result. Evaluators should make every effort to gain the competence directly or through the assistance of others who possess the required expertise.
3. Evaluators should continually seek to maintain and improve their competencies, in order to provide the highest level of performance in their evaluations. This continuing professional development might include formal coursework and workshops, self-study, evaluations of one's own practice, and working with other evaluators to learn from their skills and expertise.

C. Integrity/Honesty: Evaluators ensure the honesty and integrity of the entire evaluation process.
1. Evaluators should negotiate honestly with clients and relevant stakeholders concerning the costs, tasks to be undertaken, limitations of methodology, scope of results likely to be obtained, and uses of data resulting from a specific evaluation. It is primarily the evaluator's responsibility to initiate discussion and clarification of these matters, not the client's.
2. Evaluators should record all changes made in the originally negotiated project plans, and the reasons why the changes were made. If the changes would significantly affect the scope and likely results of the evaluation, the evaluator should inform the client and other important stakeholders in a timely fashion (barring good reason to the contrary, before proceeding with further work) of the changes and their likely impact.

3. Evaluators should seek to determine, and where appropriate be explicit about, their own, their clients', and other stakeholders' interests concerning the conduct and outcomes of an evaluation (including financial, political, and career interests).

4. Evaluators should disclose any roles or relationships they have concerning whatever is being evaluated that might pose a significant conflict of interest with their role as an evaluator. Any such conflict should be mentioned in reports of the evaluation results.

5. Evaluators should not misrepresent their procedures, data, or findings. Within reasonable limits, they should attempt to prevent or correct any substantial misuses of their work by others.

6. If evaluators determine that certain procedures or activities seem likely to produce misleading evaluative information or conclusions, they have the responsibility to communicate their concerns, and the reasons for them, to the client (the one who funds or requests the evaluation). If discussions with the client do not resolve these concerns, so that a misleading evaluation is then implemented, the evaluator may legitimately decline to conduct the evaluation if that is feasible and appropriate. If not, the evaluator should consult colleagues or relevant stakeholders about other proper ways to proceed (options might include, but are not limited to, discussions at a higher level, a dissenting cover letter or appendix, or refusal to sign the final document).

7. Barring compelling reason to the contrary, evaluators should disclose all sources of financial support for an evaluation and the source of the request for the evaluation.

D. Respect for People: Evaluators respect the security, dignity and self-worth of the respondents, program participants, clients, and other stakeholders with whom they interact.

1. Where applicable, evaluators must abide by current professional ethics and standards regarding risks, harms, and burdens that might be engendered to those participating in the evaluation; regarding informed consent for participation in evaluation; and regarding informing participants about the scope and limits of confidentiality. Examples of such standards include federal regulations about protection of human subjects, or the ethical principles of such associations as the American Anthropological Association, the American Educational Research Association, or the American Psychological Association. Although this principle is not intended to extend the applicability of such ethics and

standards beyond their current scope, evaluators should abide by them where it is feasible and desirable to do so.

2. Because justified negative or critical conclusions from an evaluation must be explicitly stated, evaluations sometimes produce results that harm client or stakeholder interests. Under this circumstance, evaluators should seek to maximize the benefits and reduce any unnecessary harms that might occur, provided this will not compromise the integrity of the evaluation findings. Evaluators should carefully judge when the benefits from doing the evaluation or in performing certain evaluation procedures should be foregone because of the risks or harms. Where possible, these issues should be anticipated during the negotiation of the evaluation.

3. Knowing that evaluations often will negatively affect the interests of some stakeholders, evaluators should conduct the evaluation and communicate its results in a way that clearly respects the stakeholders' dignity and self-worth.

4. Where feasible, evaluators should attempt to foster the social equity of the evaluation so that those who give to the evaluation can receive some benefits in return. For example, evaluators should seek to ensure that those who bear the burdens of contributing data and incurring any risks are doing so willingly, and that they have full knowledge of, and maximum feasible opportunity to obtain any benefits that may be produced from the evaluation. When it would not endanger the integrity of the evaluation, respondents or program participants should be informed if and how they can receive services to which they are otherwise entitled without participating in the evaluation.

5. Evaluators have the responsibility to identify and respect differences among participants, such as differences in their culture, religion, gender, disability, age, sexual orientation, and ethnicity, and to be mindful of potential implications of these differences when planning, conducting, analyzing, and reporting their evaluations.

E. Responsibilities for General and Public Welfare: Evaluators articulate and take into account the diversity of interests and values that may be related to the general and public welfare.

1. When planning and reporting evaluations, evaluators should consider including important perspectives and interests of the full range of stakeholders in the object being evaluated. Evaluators should carefully consider the justification when omitting important value perspectives or the views of important groups.

2. Evaluators should consider not only the immediate operations and outcomes of whatever is being evaluated, but also the broad assumptions, implications and potential side effects of it.

3. Freedom of information is essential in a democracy. Hence, barring compelling reason to the contrary, evaluators should allow all relevant stakeholders to have access to evaluative information and should actively disseminate that information to stakeholders if resources allow. If different evaluation results are communicated in forms that are tailored to the interests of different stakeholders, those communications should ensure that each stakeholder group is aware of the existence of the other communications. Communications that are tailored to a given stakeholder should always include all important results that may bear on interests of that stakeholder. In all cases, evaluators should strive to present results as clearly and simply as accuracy allows so that clients and other stakeholders can easily understand the evaluation process and results.

4. Evaluators should maintain a balance between client needs and other needs. Evaluators necessarily have a special relationship with the client who funds or requests the evaluation. By virtue of that relationship, evaluators must strive to meet legitimate client needs whenever it is feasible and appropriate to do so. However, that relationship can also place evaluators in difficult dilemmas when client interests conflict with other interests, or when client interests conflict with the obligation of evaluators for systematic inquiry, competence, integrity, and respect for people. In these cases, evaluators should explicitly identify and discuss the conflicts with the client and relevant stakeholders, resolve them when possible, determine whether continued work on the evaluation is advisable if the conflicts cannot be resolved, and make clear any significant limitations on the evaluation that might result if the conflict is not resolved.

5. Evaluators have obligations that encompass the public interest and good. These obligations are especially important when evaluators are supported by publicly generated funds; but clear threats to the public good should never be ignored in any evaluation. Because the public interest and good are rarely the same as the interests of any particular group (including those of the client or funding agency), evaluators will usually have to go beyond an analysis of particular stakeholder interests when considering the welfare of society as a whole.

SOURCE: Joint Committee on Standards for Educational Evaluation. (1994).

An Evaluation Practice Odyssey

Earlier sections of this chapter presented different evaluation activities and purposes, traced the historical unfolding of modern evaluation practice, described the most common evaluation approaches, and reviewed current ethical standards in the profession. Additionally, the previous section suggested that individual talents, research preferences, and cognitive styles of evaluators can influence evaluation practice. In this section the 20-year odyssey of the author's evaluation practice is recounted as evidence of a personal path that led to collaborative evaluation—not from some predetermined decision to evaluate this way or that but rather as a reaction to events and challenges that occurred along the way.

IN THE BEGINNING. . . .

In 1983, I was faced with the need to complete the evaluation of a 3-year program for teen mothers in the Caribbean called the Teenage Family Life Education Project (TEFLEP). The overall goal of TEFLEP was to reduce the rate of second pregnancies among unmarried teenagers. The four program objectives addressed (a) reducing infant morbidity and mortality by promoting use of the health clinics, (b) improving job prospects of participants by encouraging them to return to school or finding them employment, (c) increasing father-child bonding, and (d) promoting family planning. I inherited a massive dataset that had been compiled for 151 participating teen mothers and 35 controls. The person who initially designed the evaluation had set into motion an evaluation that required the full-time commitment of two host-country project staff who, over 3 years, completed and coded seven separate interview protocols. After a month of keypunching my way through the coded data (this was 1983, remember), I found to my chagrin that although second-pregnancy data were available for 85% of the participants, only 56% of the control group had continued in the study. Thirty-six of the 151 participants had become pregnant for the second time, but I had no way of knowing how this figure reflected on the program goal.

I also had other concerns about the evaluation design. At the time, the sponsoring government ministry very much wanted to know the extent to which this program had been effective. The pilot period was ending and the government was seriously considering assuming responsibility for continuation of the project. The U.S. sponsor, for whom I worked, wanted to know how participants, their parents, and community members perceived the program. In the design of the evaluation and development of the seven interview protocols, even though the external evaluator did take time to include questions about parenting that would further her personal research interests, she gave no thought to collecting information from the various project stakeholders that would assist in the assessment of the program.

My third concern was personal. I needed a dissertation topic. In a confluence of events, I was able to redesign the evaluation, complete it, and then use it as a case study for my dissertation, which became a meta-evaluation. As an evaluation of an evaluation, my study looked critically at the original design and then demonstrated how the redesign added useful information and was much more responsive to the stakeholders' needs.

During my doctoral work, in addition to as many research and statistics courses as I could include in my course of study, I had taken a course in educational program evaluation and was familiar with the various approaches that were then popular in the emerging discipline. My practical experience with evaluation, which began in 1974 with an international development project in Africa and extended to health and education projects in the United States, created a context within which I could weigh the information that was presented in the doctoral course. Among the evaluation approaches presented, I had gravitated most toward Stake's responsive model as the one that best mirrored my beliefs about evaluation and what it might accomplish:

> I have made the point that there are many different ways to evaluate educational programs. No one way is the right way. Some highly recommended evaluation procedures do not yield a full description nor a view of the merit and shortcoming of the program being evaluated. Some procedures ignore the pervasive questions that should be raised whenever educational programs are evaluated.
>
> Some evaluation procedures are insensitive to the uniqueness of the local conditions. Some are insensitive to the quality of the learning climate provided. Each way of evaluation leaves some things de-emphasized.
>
> I prefer to work with evaluation designs that perform a service. I expect the evaluation study to be useful to specific persons. An evaluation probably will not be useful if the evaluator does not know the interests of his audiences. During the evaluation study, a substantial amount of time may be spent learning about the information needs of the persons for whom the evaluation is being done. The evaluator should have a good sense of whom he is working for and their concerns.
>
> To be of service and to emphasize evaluation issues that are important for each particular program, I recommend the *responsive evaluation* approach. It is an approach that sacrifices some precision in measurement, hopefully to increase the usefulness of the findings to persons in and around the program.
>
> Responsive evaluations require planning and structure; but they rely little on formal statements and abstract representations, e.g., flow charts, test scores. Statements of objectives, hypotheses, test batteries, and teaching syllabi are, of course, given primary attention if they are primary components of the instructional program. Then they are treated not as the basis for the evaluation plan but as components of the instructional plan. These components are to be evaluated just as other components are. The proper amount of structure for responsive evaluation depends on the program and persons involved (Stake, 1983, 291-292).

I used House's (1978) evaluation model framework to set the stage for the logic of Stake's (1983) responsive evaluation approach. House's eight elements listed systems analysis, behavioral objectives, decision making, goal free, art criticism, accreditation, adversary, and transaction as the key evaluation approaches of the time. I argued that the TEFLEP external evaluator had very narrowly equated evaluation with the behavioral objectives approach and had thereby ignored important decision-making and transactional components required for the evaluation. I found support for this argument in Guba and Lincoln's *Effective Evaluation* (1981). Guba and Lincoln acknowledged that their work had been influenced by Stake's, and although they strongly promoted qualitative approaches in naturalistic settings as best suited to the evaluation of education programs, they allowed that "There are times, however, when the issues and concerns voiced by audiences require information that is best generated by more conventional methods, especially quantitative methods" (p. 36).

I redesigned the TEFLEP evaluation, expanding it to include interviews with relevant stakeholders: advisory council members, TEFLEP staff, ministry coordinators, community representatives, participants, and their parents. This redesign provided the information the sponsoring agencies needed to make decisions about program expansion and participants' satisfaction. I solved the second-pregnancy measurement dilemma by identifying an equivalent cohort of teens in the geographic area who had delivered their first babies a year before the TEFLEP program began and were therefore ineligible for participation. The retrospective sample allowed me to report that the second-pregnancy rate of 24% among TEFLEP participants compared very favorably to the 48% second-pregnancy rate among the comparison group for an equivalent 3-year period. Thus responsive evaluation provided a framework for my dissertation and support for my evaluation practice.

IN THE MIDDLE. . . .

In 1985, I began working at the University of North Carolina at Greensboro (UNCG) as a visiting assistant professor in the educational research area. I was hired to teach the graduate educational program evaluation course and some of the introductory educational research courses. In 1986, Dick Jaeger and I were grappling with a program evaluation design, and Dick suggested that we invite Bob Stake, Ernie House, and Kathryn Hecht to collaborate. I had, of course, heard Stake speak at professional meetings but was delighted at the prospect of actually working with him and getting to know him. In the course of collaboratively developing a modular evaluation design with the group (Jaeger, O'Sullivan, Hecht, House, & Stake, 1986), I added new ideas and practices to my evaluation toolkit. I also discovered that the real Bob Stake had more dimensions than the Stake whose work had informed my understanding of evaluation and dissertation. I was most struck by his insistence on making the components of the proposed evaluation meaningful to the clients. To do this, he designed a graphic that demonstrated how each of the evaluation modules fit within the context of the program. It was not something I would have thought to do. It measurably strengthened the evaluation design and imprinted on me the importance of client understanding in the evaluation process.

During the next few years, now as an assistant professor of educational research at UNCG, my contact with Bob continued. He came to UNCG to do a short course on case study methods and on another occasion to a May 12th Group Evaluation meeting. The following year, he invited me to a May 12th Group Evaluation meeting that he hosted at the University of Illinois that focused on issues surrounding classroom assessment. Through those contacts, my understanding of evaluation expanded and matured. I developed a deeper appreciation for the importance of qualitative methods in general and their particular importance to evaluators who care to be responsive to clients' needs. The inquiry into classroom assessment caused me to remember the important role that evaluators play in questioning topical educational policy areas beyond our clients' immediate intents. Evaluators need to be responsive to the public's needs as well.

In 1990, I had a research leave from UNCG for a semester, and to my delight, it coincided with Bob and Bernadine Stake's spending a semester at UNCG. Bob was slated to teach his course in case study methods, and I had the luxury and pleasure of participating as a student. Had I been able to travel during my research leave, one of my first thoughts would have been to go to the University of Illinois and study with Bob. As events unfolded, I expanded my skills and Bob and Bernadine came to know my family better. The case study class was a learning experience from a variety of perspectives. Although I had had Bob's short course in case study methods, the semester-long contact appreciably advanced my understanding of qualitative research methods in general and case study methods in particular. Extended contact with Bob and Bernadine proved to be the ideal research leave for me.

Within the next year, I developed and introduced a course in case study methods at UNCG. Within our educational research area at UNCG, the only course in which students encountered qualitative methods was in my educational program evaluation. Students sorely lacked the training they needed to use the qualitative methods that interested them. By default, I had become the informal qualitative methods person in the department. Luckily, an undergraduate degree in anthropology supported this designation along with my years of experience using qualitative methods in evaluations. The case study course with Bob bolstered my knowledge and my confidence in conducting qualitative inquiries.

In terms of my evaluation practice, the strengthening of my qualitative skills was accompanied by a deeper appreciation of responsive evaluation. Responsiveness was not just listening to a program's evaluation needs but also anticipating the audiences' levels of evaluation expertise and depicting the results in ways that enhanced their understanding. Often, this also meant that the evaluator's job was to reflect the program back to the audiences in intelligible ways; the audiences could decide about the merit. There was much merit in naturalistic generalizations (Stake, 1978).

BEYOND THE MIDDLE. . . .

The expansion of responsive evaluation to include audience understanding of evaluation findings has led me for the past 8 years to focus on collaborative evaluation. Because the term is often used interchangeably with participatory and empowerment evaluation (the topical interest group within the American Evaluation Association is called Collaborative, Participatory, and Empowerment Evaluation), let me define my intent. I prefer the term *collaborative* because it implies that people share responsibility and decision making. When stakeholders are asked to provide information for evaluations, technically they are participating in that evaluation, but they are not necessarily collaborators in the evaluation design. Similarly, program participants are usually not program collaborators in determining the content or direction of the program. I therefore prefer the term collaborative evaluation rather than participatory evaluation. To the extent that it is possible, my intent is that program staff and other stakeholders should be considered part of the evaluation team. The other side of this coin is that the evaluator should be considered a member of the program team. This does not relieve the evaluator of the overall responsibility for conducting the evaluation or summarizing evaluation results. My assumption is that evaluators are engaged because of the expertise they bring to the endeavor and that leadership for the evaluation resides in that role. Providing leadership in the technical aspects of evaluation, however, does not mean having the final say in how the evaluation unfolds. I believe that collaborative evaluation is a negotiated event, as are most true collaborations. Another distinction between collaborative evaluation and (say) empowerment evaluation is that although collaborative evaluation is empowering for participants, it is a valuable positive outcome of the process but not a component of the process as described by Fetterman, Kaftarian, and Wandersman (1996).

I view the collaborative evaluation approach that I use as a natural progression from responsive evaluation. Not only does the evaluation need to be responsive to the program's needs; it also should be responsive to the needs of the stakeholders (the evaluation should be useful to them) and the needs of the community (the people should be informed). Thus evaluators can improve the general state of evaluation by taking every opportunity to enhance clients' ability to appreciate, understand, and conduct evaluations. This is not just conceptually sound but practically useful as well.

I am well aware of the debate in the field about appropriateness of evaluators' roles (O'Sullivan, 1995). Recently I have also considered Scriven's (1996) objections to collaborative evaluation and the potential cooptation of the evaluator, as familiarity with programs and program staff increases. Yet usually the advantages gained in program awareness, staff cooperation, access to information, quality of information gathered, and enhanced receptivity to findings far outweigh the potential for (not the presence of) biased findings.

As a direct outgrowth of my belief in the strength of the responsive evaluation approach, I have opted for collaborative evaluation. How this translates into my practice is that I design evaluations that engage clients in the evaluation. The level of engagement varies by program evaluation purpose and client, but generally I seek evaluations where clients want to collaborate in the process. I also find, in the light of limited evaluation funds, that when clients are collaborators in the process, more thorough evaluation is possible.

My evaluation odyssey continues as I explore and refine my practice with more programs to evaluate across a variety of venues. As I first developed my collaborative evaluation practice, the uniqueness of what we were doing was most apparent. This included orchestrating "evaluation fairs" that were built on collaborative evaluation planning and working with program staff as evaluation team members. More recently, I have found that the elements of my collaborative evaluation practice closely parallel the elements of other evaluation approaches. I meet with clients, clarify program intents and scopes, identify evaluation purposes, design and implement evaluations, and then summarize the evaluation findings. What is singularly different, in contrast, about collaborative practice is *how* these elements are implemented. Because of the collaborative groundwork, data collection efforts that others describe as difficult are relatively straightforward. Levels of participation and cooperation that others find challenging are relatively easy to ensure. I look forward to seeing my clients, and they happily acknowledge my contribution to their work. At this juncture, I am ready to share my practice with others in the hope that they will find similar results.

2

Collaborative Evaluation as an Evaluation Approach

Introduction

Collaborative evaluation engages key program stakeholders actively in the evaluation process. Unlike distanced evaluation, in which evaluators have little or no contact with program staff, collaborative evaluation deliberately seeks involvement from all program stakeholders during all stages of the evaluation. A collaborative stance can strengthen evaluation results and increase the use of evaluation findings. Additionally, programs participating in collaborative evaluations may develop an enhanced capacity to consume and conduct evaluations, and evaluators may gain a better understanding of the program. The collaborative evaluation approach described in this book builds on an "evaluation voices" perspective that combines aspects of cluster evaluation with collaborative consensus models of community development. Further, the approach assumes that evaluation expertise within programs is developmental, and thus the degree of collaboration must vary by the nature and readiness of the program. Evaluations completed with this collaborative approach have yielded improved data quality, report writing, and evaluation use with programs in the areas of education, social services, and health; I also have found that collaborative evaluation may increase the resources available to the evaluation.

This chapter explains my definition of collaborative evaluation as distinct from other variants of the participant evaluation approach presented in chapter 1 and then presents a brief description of evaluation voices, one conceptualization of collaborative evaluation, which works well with multiple programs of similar intent. Next, the chapter contains a description of some common collaborative evaluation practices that have emerged as generally useful to almost all collaborative evaluation efforts. The section that follows details important signposts that collaborative evaluators should notice when determining appropriate levels of collaboration around evaluation. Finally, the chapter ends with a description of a 6-year program evaluation that greatly stimulated and served as a field-test site for the development of the collaborative evaluation approach.

Collaborative Evaluation

Chapter 1 presented six different approaches to evaluation, of which the last named was the participant approach. Within the participant approach, a number of variants has emerged since the 1960s. For example, Stake (1983) promoted "responsive evaluation," Lincoln and Guba (1985) "naturalistic inquiry," Patton (1997) "utilization-focused evaluation," and Fetterman (1994) "empowerment evaluation." Although they are distinct from one another, each of these approaches falls within the participant approach, as they all promote the inclusion of essential stakeholders in the evaluation process.

"Collaborative evaluation," my personal preference, also falls within the participant approach, but as the term is widely used with different meanings, some discussion of terms is warranted. In current evaluation parlance, *collaborative* evaluation may be used interchangeably with *participatory* or *empowerment* evaluation. The American Evaluation Association Topical Interest Group that unites evaluators who are interested in this area is called Collaborative, Participatory, and Empowerment Evaluation. Cousins and colleagues (Cousins, Donohue, & Bloom, 1996; Cousins & Earl, 1992, 1995; Cousins & Whitmore, 1998) have done considerable work in the area of collaborative and participatory evaluation. They defined collaborative evaluation as "any evaluation in which there is a significant degree of collaboration or cooperation between evaluators and stakeholders in planning and/or conducting the evaluation" (Cousins et al., 1996, p. 210). Cousins and Earl (1992, 1995) described participatory evaluation as applied social research wherein evaluators train key program staff to work with them on the evaluation. I do not personally agree with these definitions but offer them here as evidence that terminology in the field is under development.

Cousins and Whitmore (1998) used the term *collaborative* as the broadest umbrella, under which they include participatory evaluation as one of three possible approaches. They identify two participatory evaluation approaches (practical and transformative), other collaborative evaluation approaches (e.g., stakeholder-based evaluation, empowerment evaluation), and other forms of collaborative inquiry (e.g., participatory action research, cooperative inquiry) under the collaborative umbrella and seek to examine similarities and differences across three dimensions of collaborative inquiry (i.e., control of decision making, selection for participation, and depth of participation).

Another way to frame the discussion is to observe that some collaborative approaches focus on making evaluations feasible and enhancing evaluation utilization, and others emphasize the importance of empowering participants. Fetterman (2001) pointed out that strong overlaps in practice exist among the three terms (collaborative, participatory, and empowerment evaluation) and sees this overlap as positive. For him, collaborative covers the broadest range of activities. He argues that empowerment differs from participatory evaluation (as represented by Brunner & Guzman, 1989) on the dimension of stakeholder control, with empowerment evaluation assuming greater stakeholder control than participatory evaluation. In fact, empowerment evaluation assumes that stakeholders will assume leadership of the evaluation process. In contrast, Cousins and Earl (1992, 1995) maintain that with participatory evaluation, the external evaluator should lead the evaluation. In yet another slant on the topic, Patton (1997) asserts in his principles of participatory evaluation that "The evaluator is a facilitator, collaborator, and learning resource; participants are decision makers and evaluators" (p. 100). All three of these stakeholder-based evaluation approaches emphasize the importance of including various stakeholder audiences in the evaluation; they differ in who provides leadership and who ultimately makes the final decisions about the evaluation. The collaborative evaluation approach described in this book takes a stance somewhat different from the three above. It views the issue from a responsive evaluation perspective. Thus, leadership for the evaluation and final decision making authority will vary depending on a program's evaluation needs and demands.

The collaborative approach described in this chapter evolved during the last 15 years of my evaluation practice (O'Sullivan, 1999b). What was initially a responsive evaluation orientation (Stake, 1983) gradually progressed into a collaborative evaluation stance. Following Stake's logic that evaluations should be responsive to program needs, I encountered different evaluation situations that required different evaluation strategies. Some programs needed advice with evaluation planning; others wanted to find out about outcome attainment; others wanted an evaluation but were not sure what that actually meant. Responsive evaluation dictated that evaluation designs adapt to meet these differences. On occasion, the responsive evaluations would come in the wake of unresponsive evaluations, and the effectiveness of the former was demonstrated time and again (see, for example, O'Sullivan, 1984).

Not only did experience show that the evaluations needed to be responsive to the programs' needs; it also demonstrated that they needed to be responsive to communities that ultimately needed people with expertise in evaluation. Programs presented real differences in evaluation readiness and expertise. Some programs resisted evaluation; others only did evaluation because their sponsor demanded it. In some instances, the evaluation expertise on staff was not sufficient to successfully engage an external evaluator. If program evaluators did not engage program staff, little change could be expected in the organization's capacity to conduct subsequent evaluations. Collaboration with program staff seemed in order.

Finally, theory and practice combined to show that too often, evaluation studies went unread, misunderstood, or unheeded. In some programs, staff did not see the relevance of evaluation questions posed by funders and would not even read the report. On occasion, reports were overly technical in nature and beyond the understanding of program staff. In other instances, program developers new to data-driven decision making decided to ignore evaluation findings because it was easier or did not suit their beliefs. Similar events occurred when evaluators failed to gain the confidence of the program staff. Collaborative evaluation was a strategy to meet these new experiences and logically extend the responsive approach.

Collaborative evaluation, as defined here, encompasses a host of practices that are intended to engage program stakeholders in evaluation. The term *collaboration* implies that people share responsibility for the evaluation, including decision making. At the same time, there is no preordained determination of leadership or responsibility. When stakeholders are asked to provide information for evaluations, technically they are participating in that evaluation, but they are not necessarily collaborators in the evaluation. In the same way that program participants are usually not program collaborators in determining the content or direction of the program, program staff members in a participatory evaluation may or may not determine the direction of an evaluation. In the extreme, some nondirective participatory evaluations are stalemated, and no one determines the direction of the evaluation. Thus it appears to me that collaborative evaluation, rather than participatory evaluation, implies a varying level of involvement that considers the extent to which program staff and other stakeholders should be included as part of the evaluation team. They bring important program knowledge and insights to any evaluation activity, and to the degree that they are able and willing, they need to be encouraged to participate in the process. The participation of program staff in the evaluation, however, does not allow the evaluator to abrogate fundamental responsibility for the evaluation. By virtue of training and experience, the evaluator brings to the collaborative evaluation table a wealth of knowledge about evaluation strategies. With a collaborative approach, the program, participant, and evaluation expertise all need to be honored and encouraged to contribute to the evaluation process as much as is feasibly possible.

Collaborative evaluation is often empowering to participants. It enhances their understanding of evaluation so that they gain new skills. As such, it is a valuable positive outcome of the process, but not an intended one as described by Fetterman et al. (1996) or Burke (1998).

Collaborative evaluation also promotes utilization of evaluation findings. Utilization of evaluation findings continues to be a central problem in the field (Ciarlo, 1981; Patton, 1986; Smith, 1988; Stevens & Dial, 1994). Patton (1997) would probably argue that it is *the* problem in the field. Some assert that the evaluator should be the person responsible for promoting evaluation use (Chelimsky, 1986; Cousins et al., 1996; Knott, 1988; Mowbray, 1988; Weiss, 1998). I and others (Fetterman et al., 1996; Greene, 1987; Guba & Lincoln, 1989; Levin, 1996; Linney & Wandersman, 1996; Patton, 1988) believe that involving stakeholders in the evaluation process will improve evaluation utilization.

Program staff members may ignore evaluation findings because they do not understand them or have not been involved directly in the planning and implementation of the evaluation process. Distanced evaluators, conducting distanced evaluations, fail to engage program stakeholders in the evaluation and thereby limit the potential for the findings to positively influence the program. Logically, if program personnel are collaboratively involved in the evaluation, their use and understanding of the findings should increase.

Collaborative evaluation approaches have long been controversial in the field (O'Sullivan, 1995). Traditionally, evaluators have debated the appropriateness of roles that involve evaluators directly with program staff, and collaborative evaluators question the relevance and effectiveness of distanced evaluations. More recently, Stufflebeam (1994) debated Fetterman (1995) about the value of empowerment evaluation. Scriven (1996) raised objections to collaborative evaluation and the potential cooptation of the evaluator as familiarity with programs and program staff increases.

Until recently, Scriven has cast collaborative evaluation as evaluation consulting rather than actual evaluation. Yet in many instances, program staff in collaborative evaluation can be considered extensions of the evaluation team. As such, they bring to the evaluation effort different levels of expertise that the team leader recognizes and incorporates into evaluation assignments. From a management perspective, strengthening evaluation skills among team members is an extremely desirable practice. Most evaluators who engage in collaborative evaluation believe that the advantages gained in program awareness, staff cooperation, access to information, quality of information gathered, and enhanced receptivity to findings far outweigh the potential for (not the presence of) biased findings (Fetterman, 1995, Fetterman et al., 1996; Levin, 1996; Patton, 1997).

The number and types of collaborative and participatory evaluation approaches expand and the accumulation of evidence supporting the approach grows (King, 1998). Much of the literature focusing on participatory evaluation shares lessons learned from the field (see, for example, Coupal & Simoneau, 1998; Gaventa, Creed, & Morrissey, 1998). In one study, O'Sullivan and D'Agostino (1998, 2002) presented empirical evidence that a collaborative evaluation approach contributed to improved evaluation reporting. This expanding body of evidence is encouraging, but more data are needed.

I practice collaborative evaluation by designing evaluations that engage clients in the process. The level of engagement varies by program evaluation purpose and client. In some situations, however, collaborative evaluation is not the best approach. In these instances, the purpose of the evaluation is the overriding guide to the selection of evaluation approaches. Generally, however, a collaborative stance that respects clients and stakeholders will fare better than an approach that does not.

Evaluation Voices: A Type of Collaborative Evaluation

The collaborative evaluation approach may have a number of variants. "Evaluation voices" (O'Sullivan & O'Sullivan, 1994, 1998) is one conceptualization of collaborative evaluation that works well with multiple programs of similar intent. It combines the elements of cluster evaluation with collaborative consensus models of community development. Cluster evaluation was created (Kellogg Foundation, 1991) to strengthen the evaluation expertise among similar programs, thereby better meeting funders' needs for program evaluation information. The literature supports the idea that many positive gains in evaluation occur (e.g., identifying consensus around overarching program outcomes, sharing common data-gathering instruments, and enhancing professional resource networks) as the result of cluster networking activities (Barley & Jenness, 1993; Henry, 1992; Jenness & Barley, 1992; Mansberger, 1993; Pearl & Rubino, 1993; Seefeldt, 1992). "Community voices" (Callaway, Arnold, & Norman, 1993) was a leadership development program aimed at fostering community problem solving among limited resource communities; the community voices process points the way to active participation among constituents. Evaluation voices combines these two approaches, enabling program personnel to strengthen their ability to critically evaluate program effects.

Evaluation voices assumes that programs with similar goals can strengthen their evaluation strategies through cluster networking and must build evaluation expertise from within. To accomplish this, evaluators from different programs with similar intents meet to focus on a process that (a) begins with program staff and stakeholders sharing their vision for the program, (b) recognizes the current level of evaluation skill present within programs, (c) identifies barriers to strengthening evaluation, (d) provides training to overcome the identified barriers to evaluation, and (e) generates an action plan to determine the next steps in the evaluation process. Conceptually, evaluation voices assumes that effective evaluation is an ongoing activity that spirals through a consistent process of (a) perceiving a vision for the program, (b) forming evaluation questions relevant to that vision, (c) designing and implementing an information system to help answer those questions, and (d) summarizing the information collected so that the vision for the program may be revisited. Although this may resemble a typical evaluation sequence, the process of sharing individual experiences within the group over time promotes more thoughtful practice.

For programs attempting to address similar goals and objectives (i.e., career education, minority health issue awareness, sustainable agriculture), the use of evaluation voices can forge evaluation partnerships that yield stronger evaluation inquiries and results. Further, the approach can facilitate consolidation of and consensus on common program outcomes.

Particularly Collaborative Practices

Evaluation voices is one type of collaborative evaluation; many others are possible. Within these different types, certain practices are common and particularly serve to facilitate collaboration. At each juncture of an evaluation, a collaborative stance promotes stakeholder involvement. Above all, such an approach works diligently to communicate with program staff about the evaluation. At first glance, some of these techniques appear identical to traditional evaluation practice. The emphasis on stakeholder engagement at each juncture, however, separates these practices from more traditional methods and promotes positive engagement with the evaluation.

The key collaborative practices are listed here with short descriptions to provide an overview. They are explained in more detail in subsequent chapters of this book.

Responses to the Evaluation Requests. A collaborative approach requires that evaluators spend adequate amounts of time understanding the program and the evaluation purpose. This will be evaluators' first contact with the program, and the possibility for miscommunication is high. Collaborative evaluators understand the importance of gathering initial information and probing potential evaluation purposes.

Framework for a Proposal. Developing a complete evaluation proposal provides a dynamic way for evaluators to communicate their understanding of the program and the evaluation needs; ensuing dialogue is very useful. In particular, using an *evaluation crosswalk* to generate evaluation questions that are coupled with proposed data collection methods is another powerful way to engage stakeholders in the evaluation design phase. Cross-referencing questions with data sources yields more realistic assessments of appropriateness and feasibility than evaluation questions alone.

Evaluation Fairs, Conferences, and Showcases. Events such as these can create opportunities for program staff to share program accomplishments. They also have proven to be excellent ways to promote quality evaluation practices, reinforce the need for evaluation planning, and enhance program networking. Furthermore, these practices can be useful in other evaluation settings, not just the collaborative.

Identifying Levels of Collaboration

Collaborative evaluators need to design and conduct evaluations that are responsive to the organization's culture surrounding evaluation, staff's readiness to conduct evaluation, available evaluation resources, and evaluators' and clients' desired level of involvement. This section describes the signposts evaluators seek for each of these areas as they identify the appropriate levels of collaboration.

EVALUATION CULTURE WITHIN AN ORGANIZATION

An organization and the individuals who work within that organization bring with them a long and varied history of evaluation experience. These experiences blend with how their agency is organized and operated to create an evaluation culture that will influence how evaluators are received and will indicate the extent to which evaluators are able to design and implement collaborative evaluations. Further, the evaluation context and the interaction of evaluation purposes with organizational factors will influence the degree to which collaborative evaluation can be implemented.

PREVIOUS EVALUATION HISTORY

Almost everyone can recall a time when they filled out a meaningless form, answered questions about their program asked by people who knew little about the effort, provided evaluation information that they never saw summarized, or read evaluation reports that they considered useless. In some cases, people also can recall very unpleasant evaluation experiences that make them extremely reluctant to participate in evaluation again. Recognizing that program staff members may associate evaluation with something meaningless or aversive attunes evaluators to some of the possible barriers that may present resistance to evaluation.

ORGANIZATIONAL CLIMATE

Organizations operate in different ways, follow the lead of administrators with different leadership styles, and function under different conditions and circumstances. Just as organizational culture will influence how evaluation is viewed and accepted, organizational climate will temper people's willingness to participate in evaluation. This situation is true for all evaluation but is of particular importance in collaborative evaluations. Collaborative evaluators want organizations to participate as fully as possible in the evaluation efforts. An agency with a leader who discourages collaboration within the office on programmatic issues is likely to prove more difficult to engage in collaborative evaluation than an agency in which the organization normally operates collaboratively and staff members actively participate in decision making.

DOCUMENTATION

Axiom: The level of documentation that an organization keeps is always "just right" for them—no matter how little or how much it may be.

Corollary: No organization *wants* to collect more information than is currently being collected; they need to be convinced.

Organizational culture also includes an agency's "paperwork" ethic, which can vary greatly. Some people are surprised to learn that certain small groups keep no records at all. Members of these organizations consider their engagement in the work as more than sufficient evidence that they are doing a quality job. Others, on the other hand, keep copious amounts of information about their activities and outcomes. Some agencies, in fact, observe that they are drowning in paper, which keeps them from actually providing the needed documentation or information. The level of documentation at an agency will influence its readiness for collaborative evaluation. Thus evaluators must become aware of the amount and types of documents an organization compiles.

Evaluation Context

Beyond previous evaluation history and agency organization, the evaluation context will determine how program staff view evaluation. If the purpose of the evaluation is politically motivated (for example, because someone wanted to eliminate a program or a person), then this evaluation context will influence how the evaluation unfolds. Even without hidden motives and purposes, evaluation can be a psychologically threatening event for program staff. Evaluation implies judgment, and people are often uncomfortable with others judging their work. Emotions from apprehension to fear can accompany an evaluation, and evaluators must recognize these sentiments and find ways to respond to these concerns.

IDENTIFYING A PROGRAM STAFF'S READINESS FOR EVALUATION

Overall, to conduct successful evaluations, evaluators must determine the readiness level that program staff members bring to the joint evaluation endeavor. For any agency, the organizational culture around evaluation is influenced by previous evaluation history, organizational climate, and evaluation context; an evaluator must assess these dynamics and proceed accordingly. Identifying a program staff's evaluation readiness facilitates this process.

As with most readiness assessments, the process is developmental: People move from one level to the next, rarely skip steps, and often regress to previous levels when they are under stress. The following is a "weather report" that presents the evaluation readiness that evaluators may find within a program.

Reluctant to Go Outside

In this response, evaluators may find that staff believe evaluation is something imposed from outside, a waste of time, or threatening to the program. Staff may believe that evaluation keeps the program from providing valuable services or that keeping records is unnecessary. Evaluators may hear such statements as, "I know that our program is working" and "See the bags under my eyes? I know we're doing a good job."

People who are "reluctant to go outside" view evaluation as something they would rather not do. Their experience has led them to believe that evaluation is not useful; sometimes they have even experienced it as harmful. Evaluators must find ways to convince these staff members that positive outcomes can and should be the result of evaluation. Often this requires reminding people that no one wants to waste time in activities that fail to accomplish important goals, that strong evidence about a program can ensure the future of that program, and that program improvement is everyone's concern.

In a Dense Fog

Staff who are "fogged in" may feel that evaluation is a necessary evil, confusing, intimidating, or beyond understanding. They may ask, "Tell me what you want to evaluate," or state, "I don't know what I'm supposed to do." Evaluators may encounter antagonistic responses, such as "You can't measure what I want to measure" and "You can't randomly select samples with my program."

When "in a dense fog," staff members have stopped fighting the notion of evaluating the program, but they are still confused about the process. Although they see it as necessary, it is still an evil in that it takes away time from program activities. They often fail to see the value of the evaluation effort and would rather not be involved. They will collect what the evaluator demands, but no more than that. Sometimes they have accepted that evaluation activities will occur but may not see how any evaluation can measure what they are trying to accomplish.

Haze Is Lifting

As the fog lifts, staff may begin to believe that keeping records is important and that they are willing to try. They may request assistance in developing an evaluation plan or ask if the evaluator has any instruments that could be modified for their specific evaluation. Evaluators may begin to field questions such as "How can we measure success?" and "Once I get the data, what do I do with it?"

Those staff for whom the "haze is lifting" bring more enthusiasm to the process and genuinely want to learn more about evaluation. They see evaluation as something that can be useful and want assistance in finding out information about their programs. They are relatively easy to engage in a collaborative evaluation and want to share information, tools, and approaches.

On a Clear Day. . . .

When the "sky" is clear, staff may understand that they need to know how to improve the program and that evaluation can be used to answer important questions. They will believe that evaluators can provide the technical expertise to augment their evaluation capability, that internal capacity for evaluation can be increased, and that external evaluators can help them with the studies they need.

Those program staff members who see evaluation "on a clear day" truly embrace the idea that evaluation can assist them in better understanding their programs and accomplishing their goals. They often view evaluators as technical consultants who can advance their practice or improve their management. For example, they may have already collected information about the program but need technical assistance to summarize the findings. At other times, some of these program staff will view evaluators as bringing the additional assistance needed to answer evaluation questions that they themselves lack the time and expertise to pursue.

AVAILABLE EVALUATION RESOURCES

The level of collaboration possible in the evaluation also will depend on the program's available resources. Evaluators need to consider both direct and indirect resources in the assessment. Direct resources include amount of personnel time, travel, supplies, and other support budget items actually allocated to the evaluation. Indirect resources include information already being collected as a part of the program that can be used to answer evaluation questions or program personnel resources that the organization is willing to commit toward the evaluation. An assessment of both types of resources will greatly enhance an evaluator's ability to estimate the level of collaborative evaluation possible.

Finding out about direct resources can be problematic. On occasion, in a request for proposals (RFP) for an evaluation, programs will not specify the amount of funding available. They will say that they want the evaluator to give them an idea of what is needed and how much it would cost. This is not helpful to either the program or the evaluator because, more often than not, programs have already estimated the budget amount available to the evaluation. More than likely, without the estimate of available resources, the evaluators' responses to the RFP will fall short of what is desired. This situation is similar to someone inviting a contractor to his or her home for an estimate for renovations and not giving that contractor a budget figure of what the individual wants to spend. The likelihood of a reasonable estimate in both cases is slim.

Another aspect of assessing the direct resources available for the evaluation concerns the fact that programs want more evaluation than they have budgeted resources for. Until the program sets priorities and pares down the scope of the evaluation, the collaboration level will be difficult to determine. The indirect resources available for the evaluation are yet another aspect to assess that will influence the possible level of collaboration. Sometimes available indirect resources can supplement evaluation activities that would be beyond the scope of the available direct resources. For example, reports that the program generates to summarize service statistics relevant to the evaluation are indirect resources that evaluators can use. Further, some program staff may be willing to conduct focus groups or interviews, as well as assisting with other aspects of data collection.

DESIRED LEVEL OF INVOLVEMENT

Programs may vary in terms of how much involvement they seek in the evaluation. A program's desired level of involvement is the last aspect that an evaluator must explore when determining the possible level of collaboration.

An organization's culture may be very open and supportive of evaluation, but staff vacancies may have individuals so overextended that they cannot participate in the evaluation. Similarly, staff within the organization could be developmentally at the highest stages of evaluation readiness but be unable to assist in the evaluation implementation. Finally, the resources for the evaluation may be more than adequate and collaboration with program staff minimal.

An Example of Collaborative Evaluation

The collaborative evaluation approach that I use is best exemplified by the evaluation of a countywide, comprehensive, early-childhood program that I led for 6 years. The first 3 years of the evaluation are chronicled here. The program has received about $6 million annually from the state to support programs that assist families with children under 6 years old so that all children in the county are ready for school success. With that aim, the program in this particular county contracts with about 40 local agencies to provide approximately 50 different support services in the general areas of education and quality care, family support, health, translation, and transportation. The evaluation budget for this program has been about $40,000 annually.

Initially, the program director and a committee member from the evaluation advisory group visited me to discuss the possibilities for evaluation. They were in the first 18 months of operation and only 6 months into their first implementation year. The program was, and still is, politically sensitive in the state, which meant that its existence could in fact be influenced by evaluation results. The program director and committee member said that they needed to have someone evaluate the program. Upon further probing it appeared that they were interested in both setting up a monitoring system to determine the extent of program services and in collecting information across the program about accomplishments.

The evaluation challenges were impressive: the large number of agencies collaborating to provide services, the large number of programs, the limited evaluation funds, the political sensitivity of the program to evaluation findings. The fact that the services received by individual children and their families could vary greatly added to these challenges. For example, one child might receive vision screening and no other services from the program; another child might receive subsidized day care in a preschool center that was working on quality enhancement supported by the program and his or her parents might receive home visits from another of the program's support services.

This evaluation dilemma was similar in scope to the one I had faced 12 years earlier, evaluating the teen pregnancy prevention program in the Caribbean. To be responsive to the program's evaluation needs, I needed this time to use collaborative evaluation. Clearly, given the size of the program and the available resources to conduct the evaluation, the program contractors would have to become active participants in the evaluation. They would have to supply basic information about program services that they had provided to include with the state's mandatory quarterly reporting requirements. Beyond that, these contractors also would have to collect evaluative evidence about their program accomplishments (outcomes). The external evaluation team would need to spend time working with the contractors, set up data collection systems, and might be able to conduct a few focused studies on important evaluative outcomes (e.g., client satisfaction, quality care, parent education). The key to the success of the evaluation rested with the ability of the evaluators to engage contractors in this collaboratively evaluation process.

Luckily, I had been working on such a process (O'Sullivan & O'Sullivan, 1998) and could propose it to the program. Convincing evidence from the field had pointed toward the development of an evaluation approach that strengthened evaluation expertise from within programs to improve the likelihood that evaluation would be well used. The approach also had to consider common misgivings about evaluation among program staff and limited availability of program resources for evaluation. Evaluation voices (O'Sullivan & O'Sullivan, 1994) was developed to improve evaluation expertise among program staff using an innovative cluster networking context. Programs were clustered by interest area so that contractors with similar programs could share evaluation strategies, instruments, and concerns. This context was structured so that the participants would reconceptualize evaluation as a dynamic process that required their active participation and included peer learning.

We proposed using evaluation voices' cluster networking activities as the way to begin assessing and strengthening evaluation expertise among the program's contractors. We held evaluation cluster meetings in the first year of the evaluation to orient contractors to evaluation, share the evaluation plan, explain state reporting requirements, help them draft annual evaluation plans, and share data-gathering strategies. During these meetings and subsequent individual technical assistance visits, we emphasized the importance of finding out what they wanted to know about their contracted activities, which almost always coincided with what the program wanted to know overall.

The level of evaluation expertise varied greatly by contractor. A few programs were fairly sophisticated in their evaluation practice, and a corresponding number had really never collected service statistics before. Most were struggling through the first year of program implementation, with the usual delays in hiring, opening new facilities, launching new programs, and so on.

The state added to these first-year difficulties as it worked through its own program start-up complexities, which included changing the format of the quarterly reports three times. The first year's evaluation report (O'Sullivan, Clinton, Schmidt-Davis, & Wall, 1996) provided overall service statistics from programs, shared success stories, reported the results of a survey to identify quality care standards in the county, and began sharing information about countywide indicators of importance (e.g., infant mortality, number of day-care slots in the community, collaboration).

Building on the Year 1 activities, we began the second year of the evalua-tion by transferring the compilation of service statistics to the program office and working to strengthen contractors' evaluation plans. Evaluation voices cluster networking meetings continued as the way this strategy was imple-mented. Contractors participated in cluster workshops on evaluation plan-ning that were followed by individual technical assistance, as required. During these workshops, contractors were told that they would be asked to share interim evaluation results at an "evaluation fair," to be held midyear. During the evaluation fair, contractors would be expected to report their results by clusters to their peers. They were asked to submit a written report of midyear accomplishments at the same time. The external evaluation team members were available to assist contractors with implementation of their evaluation plans. The external evaluation team also worked with the overall program to develop parent education measures and assess collaboration, and it continued to report on important outcome measures. The evaluation fair was held and interim results were summarized. Contractors usually had one person within their organizations who was responsible for planning and implementing their evaluations. These were the individuals who worked with the external evaluation team. Following individual evaluation plans that were tied to the objectives of their grants from the organization, they might have collected information about client satisfaction, service provider or parent knowledge increases, or child-care center quality improvement. They also were responsi-ble for summarizing the data they collected and reporting it. At the end of the second year, interim evaluation results were updated and included as part of the second evaluation report (O'Sullivan, D'Agostino, Prohm, Roche, & Schmidt-Davis, 1997).

By the third year of the evaluation, the evaluation processes established during the first 2 years had taken root, and successful patterns continued. Evaluation planning occurred during the beginning of the year, with the eval-uation fair scheduled once again for midyear. Demand for external evaluation services was such that evaluation team members spent 10 to 15 hours each week at the program office providing technical assistance to contractors and staff. Most contractors saw the external evaluators as collaborators, and requests for technical assistance increased. It is not surprising that the quality of evaluation plans improved, as did the timeliness with which they were submitted. External evaluation team members also were asked to assist with data analysis for contractor- or program-collected data. Additional work continued on the identification of parent education measures and other common instruments.

Most important, the quality of the evaluation findings presented at the evaluation fair improved dramatically. The details of these improvements are chronicled elsewhere (see O'Sullivan & D'Agostino, 1998, 2002), but the importance of the findings is extremely relevant to the discussion at hand. The move toward collaborative evaluation was justified based on the assumption that such an evaluation approach would measurably improve the quality and utilization of evaluation. The empirical evidence collected, although still preliminary, strongly supports the quality improvement supposition of collaborative evaluation. Plans to test the assumption that collaborative evaluation improves utilization are underway.

The last 3 years of the evaluation saw the organization create a position for an internal evaluator who would take over the evaluation support activities that involved the contractors. The external evaluation team trained this internal evaluator and provided assistance to her when requested. In addition, they were engaged to conduct various evaluation studies that focused on countywide effects of the program, such as changes in collaborations among organizations and school readiness. During the entire 6-year period, the collaborative strategies developed and used for this program's evaluation were replicated with other program evaluations, which provided an opportunity to refine practices and test collaborative evaluation assumptions. The result represents much of the contents of this book.

Summary of Chapter Contents

This chapter presented a definition of *collaborative evaluation* as distinct from other appellations within the collaborative, participatory, and empowerment evaluation practices. The collaborative evaluation approach presented in this book encompasses practices geared to engage program stakeholders in evaluation. Moreover, the term assumes a responsibility for evaluation that is shared between evaluators and stakeholders. Unlike other approaches in the genre, determination of leadership and decision-making responsibility is dependent on the particular evaluation situation.

Evaluation voices is offered as one conceptualization of the collaborative evaluation approach presented. Evaluation voices combines aspects of cluster evaluation with community networking aspects to promote collaborative evaluation activities. It is appropriate for groups of programs with similar scopes of work.

Those common collaborative evaluation practices were described that have emerged as generally useful to almost all collaborative evaluation efforts, which include responding to evaluation requests, developing a framework for a proposal that includes an "evaluation crosswalk," and conducting evaluation fairs. Signposts were identified that collaborative evaluators should notice when determining appropriate levels of collaboration, including understanding the evaluation culture of an organization, the program staff's readiness for evaluation, the available evaluation resources, and the organization's desired level of involvement. A description was provided of a 6-year program evaluation that served as a field-test site for the development of the collaborative evaluation approach, greatly stimulating its development.

3

*Responding
Collaboratively to
Evaluation Requests*

How evaluators respond to evaluation requests determines whether they will be employed to conduct the proposed evaluations. The nature of the requests also provides them with the information they need to decide if they are even interested in conducting the evaluation. Each of the requests for evaluation in Figure 3.1 is different in scope and nature; each requires a different response. For each, however, the collaborative evaluator's initial step is to clarify the request. Too often, evaluators jump to the design phase of the evaluation without spending adequate amounts of time to fully understand what is wanted or needed. A collaborative evaluator recognizes the value of clarifying the evaluation by gathering information from the client acknowledging that a relationship of mutual understanding will strengthen the evaluation. Clarifying the request has three key elements: gathering information about the program's nature and scope, determining the purpose of the evaluation, and probing the resources available to conduct the evaluation.

This chapter reviews the most common types of evaluation requests, discusses strategies for clarifying evaluation requests, and provides suggestions for constructing appropriate responses. Constructed examples, using the three evaluation situations described, are used to illustrate the general practices suggested. For each of the three situations, this chapter presents strategies for clarifying the request, building on lessons learned from the field. Response strategies are presented for each situation, and the advantages of each response strategy are explored.

- A call comes in: The Director of the Mentoring Project, a small program, needs help with evaluation.
- The executive director of a local foundation asks for a meeting to discuss the possibility of you evaluating its Rural Economic Development Program, a regional 5-year funding program for 30 grantees.
- A request for proposal arrives soliciting a 3-year evaluation design for Volunteers Across America, an ongoing national education program.

Figure 3.1   Examples of Requests for Evaluation

Clarifying the Mentoring Project Request

The board of directors of the Mentoring Project has asked the Mentoring Project director to conduct an evaluation of the program. For the past 7 years, the program annually has paired 25 to 30 volunteer mentors with at-risk youth for the purposes of helping them stay in school and experience a positive relationship with an adult. The program has never been evaluated, and at a recent meeting, the board of directors decided it was time to do something. The director is not quite sure how to proceed, as she has not had extensive experience with evaluation. Through her local network of colleagues, she has identified and asked a local evaluator for assistance.

In general, program evaluation can be problematic for program staff. Small programs often lack the resources necessary to hire any evaluator, be it internal or external. Thus the responsibility for the evaluation is left to program or project administrators even though they may not have the time, inclination, or expertise to conduct the evaluation. Commonly, these administrators equate evaluation with program monitoring. For example, they check to see if the program has completed the proposed activities within allocated time and budget constraints, a necessary but extremely limited evaluation effort.

Some program administrators approach evaluation with virtually no previous experience. With agencies or administrators new to evaluation, the evaluator must be prepared to invest time explaining evaluation basics so that the client may knowledgeably select among possible evaluation options. Initially this may take the evaluator substantial amounts of time, but future smooth implementation of the evaluation will prove it a cost-effective strategy. The alternative is to have clients change the evaluation midprocess because their inexperience led them to unrealistic expectations. Similarly, with agencies that have had negative evaluation experiences, the evaluator must take the requisite time to work through lingering misperceptions and suspicions.

GATHERING PROGRAM INFORMATION

From novice programs to those experienced with evaluation, the evaluator's first response to any evaluation request is to gather as much information as possible about the program. Frequently, this can present a challenge. With many organizations (both large and small), little documentation may be available. Most staff enter programs to provide program services. Within some organizations, staff are so engaged in delivering program services that records keeping is left perennially on the "to-do" list. Other organizations fail to provide the rationale or the infrastructure needed for adequate record keeping. Some program people keep all their records in their heads. Although exploring details about the program may ostensibly appear as a time-intensive (and thus expensive) alternative for evaluators, the degree to which it facilitates the entire process usually justifies the investment.

Meeting with the director, and possibly the program staff, at their site is an excellent way for evaluators to orient themselves to programs. Additionally, on-site meetings allow evaluators to observe staff and equipment resources and gather copies of documentation that may be available. Opportunities to review available annual reports, project proposals, and other useful documents is essential to this step. A telephone or e-mail exchange is less desirable for document and resource identification but can accomplish the desired results of understanding the program. Should the client express an interest in previous evaluations completed by the evaluator, a meeting at the evaluator's office might be more appropriate; this way the evaluator can supply examples for the client to review.

DETERMINING THE EVALUATION PURPOSE

The evaluator's second response should be to clarify the purpose of the evaluation. Evaluation within small agencies (as well as large ones) can be fraught with hidden agendas. Some reasons for commissioning evaluations can be naive, misguided, or motivated by internal or external politics. Evaluation is not a leisure-time activity. Evaluations require resources that could be put to programmatic uses; therefore, rationales for evaluations should be thoughtful.

Clarifying this aspect of the evaluation request also can be challenging. Board members who promote evaluation or staff members who resist it may not understand that program evaluation can assume many poses. When the evaluator encounters difficulty understanding the purpose of the evaluation, an evaluation needs assessment could provide valuable information essential to focusing the evaluation request.

Such an evaluation needs assessment can be performed relatively quickly and will provide the evaluator with important information about the evaluation

---

Mentoring Project Evaluation Needs Assessment

The purpose of this sheet is to identify the most important aspects of the
Mentoring Project that you believe would benefit from evaluation. Please take a
few minutes of your time to let us know what you think our evaluation priorities
should be.

A. Your program role (please circle one):

    Board member   Staff   Mentor   Participant   Parent

B. In the space below, please list the two aspects of the mentoring project that
you think it is most important we should evaluate. For each evaluation
priority you list, explain why you think it is important.

First priority:_____

Importance?

First priority:_____

Importance?

Figure 3.2   Evaluation Needs Assessment for Mentoring Project

purpose. Figure 3.2 presents an evaluation needs assessment data gathering
form that could be used with a small program similar to the Mentoring
Project. This information could be gathered individually in written form, by
telephone, or during individual or group interviews.

Inclusion of the various stakeholder audiences is key in collaborative evaluation to determining the extent of evaluation needs. With small agencies, it is
possible to gather information from almost all the important stakeholders.
With larger groups, sampling is strongly recommended. Either the program
director or the evaluator could gather the information, summarize it fairly
quickly using content analysis (see Patton, 2002, for suggestions on conducting
content analysis), and then use it as the basis of a discussion to identify the
evaluation purpose. Most likely, the purpose of the evaluation can be clarified
through discussion with the program director and staff. Offering examples

of different types of evaluation approaches within the specific context of the program can provide sufficient information for program staff to indicate a particular evaluation preference.

Ultimately, the evaluator must weigh the rationale for conducting the evaluation against a commonsense scale that judges the logic of using scarce resources to conduct an evaluation for the purposes identified. Initially in the case of the Mentoring Project, the project director explained that the board wanted the evaluation because in the project's 7 years of operation it had never had one. The evaluator suspected a more complicated rationale, and when discussions did not yield a logical evaluation purpose, the evaluator suggested that the evaluation needs assessment be conducted. From the evaluation needs assessment, the evaluator discovered that there were some people within the agency who wanted to expand the scope of program operations, and therefore the board wanted to know how well things had been working before it considered new options.

PROBING EVALUATION RESOURCES

Finally, the evaluator must explore the resources available to conduct the evaluation. Most program staff, unfamiliar with evaluation, are also unfamiliar with the costs of conducting evaluations. Often they begin with grandiose ideas and extremely modest resources. Part of clarifying the evaluation request is to determine the extent of resources available to the evaluation. Resources may include funds that are available to the evaluator as well as on-site resources that may be used for the evaluation.

On-site resources can be extremely important to the evaluation. Expertise and material resources within the agency can offset limited monetary resources available to the evaluation. For example, the program director or staff may be able to assist with data collection and analysis, and the program may be able to provide copies, postage, or clerical assistance. Ultimately, though, the evaluator must elicit from the agency some sense of the total resources available to conduct the evaluation.

As the evaluator gains a sense of the program and understands the purpose of the evaluation, preliminary ideas about the evaluation begin to form. Those ideas must be regulated by resource constraints. In cases where the available resources are far below what is apparently needed, the evaluator's task becomes one of explaining the discrepancy to those commissioning the evaluation and helping the program set evaluation priorities. The problem of having too many evaluation resources is extremely unlikely to occur but must be addressed similarly. If there is an obvious mismatch between the evaluation desired and the available resources, some accommodation must be made. The program may consider reassessing its evaluation needs, opt to complete only a portion of the originally desired evaluation, or search until it finds the necessary additional resources.

Clarifying the Rural Economic Development Program Request

The executive director of a local foundation has worked with his board to develop a new funding strategy. Rather than competitively funding individual community development projects, the foundation has refocused its funding efforts to support clusters of projects that promote rural health and economic development within selected communities. Each year for 3 years, 10 communities in the southeastern United States will be identified and competitively awarded funds for a 3-year period. The board has made a 5-year commitment to the program, and the executive director is keen to establish and implement an evaluation before the end of the first project year. With assistance from an evaluation consultant, the executive director and program specialist have drafted a four-page evaluation prospectus and invited three evaluators to submit proposals.

GATHERING PROGRAM INFORMATION

The evaluator's first response, as with the previous Mentoring Project example, is to gather sufficient information about the program to understand its nature and scope. One advantage of a new funding effort is that announcements about the new program are usually available and describe the program in depth. In this case, after reading through the evaluation prospectus and the program materials, a face-to-face meeting with the executive director and program specialist would be the next step. During this meeting, the evaluator needs to raise any questions that remain about the program and must clarify the request for evaluation. One strategy that works well in this situation is to contrast the program of interest with a similar program that the evaluator knows. Another strategy is to reflect back to the client what the evaluator currently understands about the program. Saying something like, "It seems that in the first year the program would. . . ." This strategy allows the evaluator to elicit additional information about the program, and any misperceptions about the program harbored by the evaluator can be corrected.

A note of caution: Check assumptions about terminology. Organizations often coin terms that have meaning for them but do not necessarily parallel common usage in evaluation or other fields. A term like *needs assessment* may have one meaning for a foundation and quite another for an evaluator. In the case at hand, the foundation expressed a desire to commission a "strategic" evaluation. During a meeting with the executive director, the evaluator discovered that the foundation was using *strategic* as a way of distinguishing the external outcomes-oriented evaluation from the internal monitoring of individual grantees.

DETERMINING THE EVALUATION PURPOSE

Clarifying the purpose of the evaluation is also an important component of this evaluation. Unlike the Mentoring Project (which had proceeded for years without benefit of evaluation, and then for some unknown reason the board called for an evaluation), the evaluation purpose for the Rural Economic Development Program appears more grounded. The funding program is new, and the desire to evaluate a new program is consistent with good planning.

Clarifying the evaluation purpose vis-à-vis expectations about the program's outcomes and the timeline for the evaluation will be important for this evaluation. Program staff members, in their enthusiasm for new programs, occasionally overstate what a program may accomplish or how soon results will occur. Part of clarifying the purpose of the evaluation is to ensure that program expectations are aligned with probable realities. The first year of many programs proceeds slowly and is often fraught with difficulties; delays can and do occur. Evaluators must caution program staff that the likelihood of observing large outcome changes at the outset of a program is almost nil. Additionally, most new programs need information that will lead to program improvement. Evaluators should suggest, if it has not already been proposed, including formative evaluation (suggestions for program improvement) as a part of the initial evaluative purpose. Most likely, formative information will be more useful than outcome data in that it will allow for midcourse correction as the new program unfolds.

Similarly, evaluators should prepare program staff for the strong possibility that the program will change as it unfolds. Usually when people develop new programs, their vision carries them into implementation, but hindsight is often necessary to see clearly. This is why the evaluation of new programs needs to be particularly sensitive to capturing unintended outcomes that are both positive and negative. In discussions with the program staff, the evaluator needs to explore these other evaluation purposes. Most likely, they have not occurred to the program staff, and such information will help them clarify the evaluation purpose.

PROBING EVALUATION RESOURCES

Finally, the evaluator must explore the extent to which resources will be available to conduct the evaluation. Given that the Rural Economic Development Program has given much thought to the evaluation, it has probably given thought to the resources available for allocation to the evaluation. During discussions with the executive director, the evaluator must communicate to the foundation the extent to which their evaluation plans can be implemented in the light of available resources. Providing examples of what can be done for a set amount of money is a useful strategy; it promotes understanding about evaluation choices. For example, evaluating the impact of the grant for a given community could be estimated at approximately $5000 per community, assuming two site visits per year of 3 days duration each, which would include travel and evaluator time spent developing questions, gathering data, and writing reports. To include all 30 communities would mean that the foundation would have to set aside $150,000 for site visits. Thus the foundation may choose to reduce their expectations for the evaluation or decide to augment the allocated resources to fund all of the activities they desire.

At this juncture, the evaluator also needs to know about general fiscal arrangements that will be made with the foundation. The probable cost of the Rural Economic Development Program evaluation is greater than that for the Mentoring Project evaluation due to the expanded scope of the evaluation. Therefore, fiscal accountability and payment procedures will be more important. If the evaluator works for a university or private consulting firm, overhead rates (the costs of doing business for the evaluator, such as rent, utilities, accountant) will need to be discussed and included in the budget. Some foundations will not pay overhead costs directly. If true, overhead must be integrated into other cost items. Some agencies work on a cost reimbursement basis only; the evaluator will need to plan how to cover initial costs. Frequency of financial reporting is also important. The evaluator will need to consult with the foundation so that financial accounting and reporting requirements are explicit.

Clarifying the Volunteers Across America Request

Volunteers Across America is a federally funded, multimillion-dollar, national education project involving 250 programs across the United States. Two years after the program's inception, the federal government wanted an evaluation conducted, and a request for proposal (RFP) was published in the *Federal Register*. A synopsis of the RFP reached the evaluator's desk and seemed of interest. Ostensibly, the purpose of the 3-year evaluation was to examine how well the programs were working and what effects they were having. The deadline for submission of proposals was 6 weeks away.

GATHERING PROGRAM INFORMATION

Once again, the need to understand the program is essential to clarifying the evaluation request. In the case of Volunteers Across America, the RFP contained an enormous amount of information about the program, but only

6 weeks remained before the proposal was due. The first step in developing this evaluation proposal was to obtain a copy of the full RFP to better understand the purpose of the evaluation, view the criteria that would be used to judge the proposals, and determine what would be needed for proposal submission.

The RFP for the evaluation of Volunteers Across America was nine pages long and explained in some detail what was wanted. The RFP listed purposes of the evaluation, with short explanations; explained criteria for proposal review, including weighted points to be awarded for each criterion; and presented the outline for the proposal, which specified a 30-page limit. The RFP also indicated that the budget limit for the evaluation was $125,000 a year for the next 3 years, subject to annual appropriation and approval.

Unlike the first two evaluation requests, this RFP for evaluating Volunteers Across America already contains much information important to clarifying the evaluation. Rudimentary program information is included, evaluation purposes are identified, and resource limits are set. Additionally, the evaluator knows the criteria by which the proposals will be judged and has been given the outline for the proposal. In part, this information is provided because it is unlikely at the federal level that the evaluator will be able to meet with the program directors to discuss the evaluation. Occasionally (also common at the state level or with large foundations), bidders' conferences are held so that evaluators interested in responding to the RFP can ask questions. In this case, people interested in submitting proposals were invited to meet (at their own expense) to review the RFP and ask questions. Normally, in the interests of fairness, answers to bidders' conference questions are made available to all proposers; similar disclosures also are appropriate when individuals planning to respond to an RFP have conversations with program staff.

Usually, in federal proposals, a contact person and phone number are included and should be consulted. Even with detailed RFPs, evaluators must still work to clarify the evaluation request. As with all evaluation requests, understanding the program and its background is essential to understanding the request for an evaluation. With large programs, there are often program brochures, site descriptions, reports, and other documents readily available, and these should be consulted. Checking for a website and exploring that website provide additional avenues through which to gather information. The evaluator becomes familiar with the program so that the evaluation can be integrated into ongoing program activities. For example, if program directors come together regularly once or twice a year, an evaluator can plan on that time as an excellent information-gathering event with relatively minimum costs involved.

In the case of Volunteers Across America, the evaluator could and should consult a local program and ask about the proposed evaluation. Local programs are usually happy to be consulted about such matters and can provide a wealth of information to the evaluator. For example, local programs can share their expectations about evaluation outcomes, explain current weaknesses in the reporting systems, and identify problematic program areas. In consulting local programs, however, evaluators must exercise restraint and be sensitive to the fact that program people have limited time and do not have the same vested interest in securing and conducting the evaluation.

DETERMINING THE EVALUATION PURPOSE

As with the other two programs, the evaluation purposes of Volunteers Across America also need clarification. For the evaluator, gathering additional program background information should bring the evaluation purposes into clearer focus than at the outset. The fit between the program and the evaluation purposes should be apparent. Questions probably will occur to the evaluator as program details fall into place. At this juncture, contacting the person identified in the RFP to discuss questions is an appropriate step. Preparing the questions ahead of time will allow the telephone conversation to flow and ensure that no important questions are missed.

PROBING EVALUATION RESOURCES

Clarifying the evaluation resources available in the case of Volunteers Across America is simpler than in the first two situations. Evaluators can begin framing the evaluation with some understanding of a total monetary amount that will be available to conduct the evaluation. What is not as straightforward are the details and regulations that govern how the money is to be spent, or what is expected in terms of evaluation activities and products delivered to the client by the evaluator. How those resources must be allocated is an important component in understanding this evaluation request.

Figure 3.3 lists questions relevant to resource allocation that will be important for developing the evaluation proposal, which is the next evaluation design phase. With large evaluations, money management can become quite complex or potentially challenging. For example, if you are a small company and the project will cost $120,000 to $160,000 annually, you may be asked to work on a quarterly cost-reimbursement basis. Approximately $30,000 to $40,000 of expenditures will occur before reimbursement is made. The organization might also require that the accounts be audited annually. Evaluators need to make sure that they are aware of the organization's assumptions about "normal financial practice" and their expectations about how the evaluation contract will be managed.

Questions to Ask About Resources

1. Expenditure limitations
   a. Can equipment be purchased or leased?
   b. Can part of the work be subcontracted to others?
   c. Is overhead paid? If so, how is the overhead determined?
   d. How are payments made (advancements, cost-reimbursement, deliverables, other)?

2. Assumptions about deliverables and activities
   a. How many times is the evaluator expected to meet with the contractor?
   b. Are there program events that the evaluator is expected to attend?
   c. How many reports and interim reports are expected?
   d. How many copies of reports and interim reports will be needed?

Figure 3.3   Resource and Agency Assumptions Checklist

Summary of Chapter Contents

The size and scope of evaluations vary greatly. Each begins, however, with a request for evaluation. Evaluation requests can range from the incredibly vague to the very specific. Although almost all evaluators attempt to understand evaluation requirements to some degree, the collaborative evaluator recognizes the key importance of clarifying requests prior to deciding to get involved or developing an evaluation proposal. With collaborative evaluation, the clarification process is not a blip on the evaluator's radar screen but a deliberate exploration of the evaluator-client fit. The examples used in this chapter have demonstrated that no matter what the type of request, evaluators must clearly understand (a) the nature of the program to be evaluated, (b) the evaluation purpose, and (c) the resources available for the evaluation. The circumstances of these clarifying activities change in response to the type of evaluation and specificity of request. Successfully clarifying the evaluation request will strengthen the evaluation proposal and lead to an evaluation design that is appropriate to the program.

Chapter 3 Exercises

TEFLEP EVALUATION

The Teenage Family Life Education Project (TEFLEP) was a 3-year demonstration project jointly sponsored by a Ministry of Health, Education, and Social Affairs in a small Caribbean country and a social action agency in the United States. The purpose of the program was to delay the rising rate of second pregnancies among teenagers (13 to 16 years old). The main strategy of the program was to create a youth advocacy and support program that (a) reduced infant morbidity and mortality by convincing mothers to use government-sponsored maternal and child healthcare clinics, (b) improved job prospects among participants by encouraging them to return to school or aiding them in securing employment, (c) increased father-child bonding by encouraging fathers to provide greater economic and emotional support to their children, and (d) reduced incidences of second pregnancy by providing family planning education and supplies to both mothers and fathers.

During the 3-year project period, staff met regularly with the participants to provide counseling, information, and referrals about healthcare, family planning, continuing education, and employment opportunities. TEFLEP identified all teens 13 to 16 years old on the island who had given birth for the first time during the project's first calendar year of operation. Teen mothers were identified and recruited into the program primarily through the use of hospital records, as almost all first births were hospital managed. The program enrolled 151 teenage mothers into the program and randomly assigned an additional 35 teenage mothers to the control group. Program participants and controls were to complete enrollment, postpartum, and 6-, 12-, 18-, and 24-month follow-up interviews. By the end of the 3-year project, all but 3 of the 151 participants were active in the program to some degree, but only 18 of the controls were willing to continue their participation.

Activity

The project director has called you in at the end of the 3-year program to conduct the external evaluation. Generate a list of questions for her to clarify the evaluation.

4

Designing Collaborative Evaluations

Clarifying the evaluation requests for the three examples used in the previous chapter—the Mentoring Project, the Rural Economic Development Program, and Volunteers Across America—contributes to the collaborative evaluator's understanding of the programs to be evaluated, the purposes of the evaluations, and the resources available to conduct the evaluations. Occasionally, these efforts to clarify evaluation requests may convince the evaluator not to pursue the evaluation. Perhaps the fit is not good between the evaluator's previous experience and the program to be evaluated, or the evaluation may be so politically sensitive as to render objective findings problematic, or perhaps the resources allocated for the evaluation are seriously inadequate. Assuming the clarification process was successful and the evaluator has a grasp of the program, the evaluation purpose, and the available resources and has also confirmed the evaluator's initial interest in the evaluation, the next step is to design the evaluation by developing an evaluation proposal.

This chapter presents strategies for developing collaborative evaluation proposals, using the three requests for evaluation presented in chapter 3. As shown in Figure 4.1, an evaluation proposal usually includes a program background statement, an evaluation purpose, evaluation questions, an evaluation design, information-gathering options with evaluation questions, a timeline of important evaluation activities, a summary of personnel and organization qualifications, a budget, and possibly a presentation of the proposal to the client. A collaborative evaluation proposal recognizes these elements but organizes them in such a way as to promote collaboration. This collaborative framework to guide evaluation proposal design is summarized in Figure 4.2. First the *program background* statement summarizes the program and reflects

1. Program background statement
2. Evaluation purpose
3. Evaluation questions
4. Evaluation design
5. Information-gathering options with evaluation questions
6. Timeline of important evaluation activities
7. Summary of personnel and organization qualifications
8. Budget
9. Presentation and discussion of proposal with the client

Figure 4.1   Elements of a Evaluation Proposal

1. *Program background statement:* What is the nature of the program? What mission or purpose does it serve?
2. *Evaluation purpose:* What needs to be evaluated? What are the intended uses of the evaluation? Why evaluate this now? Why evaluate this as opposed to something else?
3. *Evaluation questions with proposed information-gathering activities:* Based on your program and evaluation purpose, what are the broad evaluation questions you would like answered? What information will you gather so that you have convincing evidence to answer your evaluation questions? Have you made sure that evaluation questions are answered with evidence from more than one source? Have you consulted the important stakeholders?
4. *Timeline of evaluation activities:* When will you gather important evidence? Who will be responsible for different evaluation activities? Have you allowed enough time to develop and pilot test instruments and surveys so that you are confident about the quality of the information that you are gathering? Have you allowed sufficient time for summarizing the information you collected and for report writing?
5. *Qualifications statement:* What are the qualifications of personnel who will conduct the evaluation and the organizational resources that will be available? What previous experience is relevant?
6. *Budget:* What will the evaluation cost? What new costs are created by implementing the evaluation? What staff resources in time, clerical, and other necessities will be used to complete the evaluation?

Figure 4.2   Framework for Designing an Evaluation

the evaluator's understanding of the program back to the client. In this way, lingering misconceptions about the program can be corrected. Describing the *evaluation purpose* is the second part of the evaluation proposal and also allows the evaluator's understanding to be reflected back to the client for refinement. Next, using the information gathered during the clarification step of the evaluation, the collaborative evaluator develops an initial set of *evaluation questions with proposed information-gathering activities* to begin discussions with the client about the direction the evaluation should take. Creating the *timeline of evaluation activities* allows the evaluator to consider the logistics of conducting the evaluation and demonstrates to the client how the evaluation will unfold. Providing the client with a *statement of qualifications* explains who will be involved, describes the available organizational resources, and introduces relevant previous experiences. Finally, the *budget* section details the costs associated with implementing the evaluation.

The evaluation proposal is a working document that promotes dialogue between evaluator and client. The proposal should be sufficiently detailed so that both the evaluator and client have a realistic picture of what the evaluation will entail. It is fair to assume that the proposal will undergo some modification; thus an overly detailed initial proposal will require more changes than one that covers only the key areas. The aim is to establish consensus about important evaluative issues. Usually, once agreement is reached on the evaluation framework, the evaluator, in collaboration with the client, develops a detailed evaluation plan from the proposal.

Developing a Program Background Statement

After the initial efforts to clarify the evaluation with the client, the evaluator should have sufficient information about the program to summarize key program activities or components. In part, this extends the evaluation clarification process, as the client can and will correct any misconceptions about the program the evaluator may still harbor. This program background statement further permits others who may provide assistance with the evaluation as consultants or data gatherers with a succinct description of the program so that they may better understand the evaluation context. Activity 4.1 illustrates the process of developing a program background statement for the Mentoring Project.

DESCRIBING THE EVALUATION PURPOSE

The purpose of the evaluation also should be included in the evaluation proposal. The proposal promotes communication between the evaluator and client and will clarify any lingering misconceptions. The purpose of the evaluation as stated in the proposal should make clear why the evaluation is necessary and should justify the expenditure of program resources.

The board of directors of the Mentoring Project has asked the Mentoring Project director to conduct an evaluation of the program. For each of the past 7 years, the program has paired 25 to 30 volunteer mentors with at-risk youth for the purposes of helping them stay in school and experience a positive relationship with an adult. The program has never been evaluated, and at a recent meeting, the board of directors decided it was time to do something. The director is not quite sure how to proceed, as she has not had extensive experience with evaluation. Through her local network of colleagues, she has identified and asked a local evaluation group for assistance.

Directions: Assume that you are part of a local evaluation group about to meet with the director. In the space below, write the three most important questions you will ask the director.

Question 1:

Question 2:

Question 3:

Activity 4.1   Developing a Program Background Statement

Theoretically, one could evaluate anything in a program. Programs might even request the expenditure of program resources for unnecessary evaluation activities; however, this would be contrary to good practice according to the AEA's *Guiding Principles for Evaluators* (1995) and the Joint Committee on Standards' *Program Evaluation Standards* (1994). Occasionally, evaluations are commissioned without careful thought about their purpose, and this usually results in findings that are never used. The rationale for the evaluation should be clear to everyone concerned.

IDENTIFYING EVALUATION QUESTIONS

Evaluation questions are the heart of an evaluation design. They guide what will occur and need to be thought out carefully. Evaluation questions should capture the essence of what needs to be evaluated. After collecting and analyzing information to answer the evaluation questions, the purpose of the evaluation should be realized and programs should be better informed about the issues that sparked the need for evaluation.

Selecting appropriate evaluation questions is sometimes difficult, both for the evaluator and for the client. One source of difficulty may be that the evaluator only partially understands the program or the evaluation purpose. Some misconceptions about the evaluation may persist beyond the evaluator's conscientious attempts to initially clarify the evaluation request. In shaping the evaluation questions, many lingering misconceptions often surface that do not emerge from the program background statement or the evaluation purpose. Another source of difficulty can be that clients only partially grasp the evaluation endeavor. Even when clients are clear about the overall purpose of the evaluation, they may have difficulty reaching the next level of specificity. For example, if the purpose of the evaluation is to determine the extent to which a particular program has met its objectives, a client may not have thought through the criteria or standards that constitute meeting the objectives. In either case, be it evaluator or client confusion, the evaluator would initially experience difficulty in framing questions and reaching consensus with the client about evaluation questions.

Developing Evaluation Questions for the Mentoring Project

The initial meeting with the director of the Mentoring Project helped the evaluator clarify the evaluation request and signaled to the evaluator that the organization had little experience with formal evaluation. The key area of confusion centered on separating outcome evaluation from monitoring. The Mentoring Project's board of directors wanted to know if their program, placing volunteer mentors with at-risk youth, was accomplishing its objectives; they were interested in program outcomes. During discussions with the director, the evaluator observed that the director really did not understand what the board wanted. According to the director, there was no need to evaluate the objectives, as they were "working to capacity and had more demands for mentors than volunteers." When pressed, the director revealed that what she wanted to evaluate was how many volunteers they had placed, the amount and type of training the volunteers had received, and how many of the at-risk

			Monitoring	Outcome Evaluation
Goals and Objectives	Activities	Results	Evidence of Activities and Their Quality	Evidence of Results

Figure 4.3   Evaluation Planning Form (Logic Model)

youth attended the program. The director wanted assistance monitoring program activities.

Anticipating difficulty with drafting the evaluation questions, the evaluator offered to assist the Mentoring Project director and her staff with completing the evaluation planning form shown in Figure 4.3, which is a logic model of the program and how the evaluation is related to program goals, activities, and results. In the first column, the program lists the goals and objectives to be met. In the second column, program staff and stakeholders state what activities they have implemented to achieve the objectives (more than one activity can be used to meet an objective, and one activity can meet multiple objectives). In the next column, program staff identify the expected results from each of the activities. This step can be difficult in that many program people know what they want to do but are less clear about what should result from the activities they implement. In the fourth column, program staff and stakeholders list the evidence they currently collect to demonstrate that the activities have occurred and how well they were implemented. In the fifth column, program staff members list the evidence they collect to show what results have been achieved. In this manner, program staff members begin to understand that (a) overall program objectives generate program activities, (b) program activities should result in some outcome, and (c) evidence must be collected to monitor program activities and quality as well as to determine outcome accomplishments. This activity assisted the Mentoring Program staff in understanding the programmatic relationship among goals and objectives, activities, results, monitoring, and outcome evaluation.

In using this activity with program personnel, the evaluator must be prepared to facilitate the process (see Brandon, 1998, for suggestions of ways to elicit participation from stakeholders). Often program personnel know what they want to do (the activities) before they are aware of why they want to do it or what should happen as a result. This explains why it is sometimes difficult to elicit statements of desired results and outcomes from program staff. They are so engaged in the activity or program that they have not stopped to reflect on what they hope to achieve. In these cases, when evaluators speak with program staff, staff members view the activity as synonymous with the outcome and do not initially see the difference.

Another problem, especially pervasive in large bureaucratic organizations, is the equating of monitoring and evaluation. In these types of organizations, staff understand that they must collect information to demonstrate that they have actually accomplished the tasks set out in the plan of work but often fail to understand that they also must gather evidence about the results of these activities. For example, they take attendance at trainings, keep telephone logs, or record minutes of meetings. Sometimes, the tracking of accomplishments even includes evaluating the quality of the activity, such as what participants gained from the training, what transpired during the telephone conversations, or what board members thought of meetings. The idea of examining the results of these activities is quite foreign.

Unfortunately, one reason that many program staff in large organizations fail to assess program outcomes is that they view evaluation as an endless stream of filling out forms for no apparent purpose. They are regularly asked to submit reports about program activities and never see how the information is summarized or may be used. Often their supervisors, who request the information from them, are caught in the same loop and are similarly unaware of the purpose of the data collection.

Completing the evaluation planning form does wonders to help program staff work through these perceptual blocks about evaluation and provides essential information that will assist the evaluator in generating meaningful evaluation questions. Further, this activity will provide more detail to the evaluator about what types of information are already being kept by an organization. Occasionally, the evaluator will discover that the organization is mired in unwieldy record-keeping systems that have overburdened personnel. Program staff will not welcome expanding evaluation activities if they perceive that they already are spending too much of their time keeping up with unused data. They will welcome someone who helps reduce the burden of an unwieldy record-keeping system.

Reluctance to engage in more evaluation can be bridged if in the proposal the evaluator suggests ways to streamline data collection. For example, one agency was working with a volunteer from the university who was helping staff collect and summarize the agency's monthly service statistics, such as the number of telephone requests, the types of responses, and so on. The university professor had them preparing data that were subsequently analyzed on the university's mainframe computer. A month or two later, the agency received pages of printout that they did not understand. The program staff spent hours each week collecting and preparing the information to send to the university. They were not pleased with the system but did not know what else to do, and they did not want to hurt the volunteer's feelings. The evaluator in this case (using as much diplomacy as possible) found another important volunteer activity for the university professor and was able to show the program staff how they could use the database program that came with their word processor to record and summarize the data they needed.

After working through the evaluation planning form with the staff of the Mentoring Project, the evaluator had a clearer idea of how to focus the evaluation. Initially program staff had difficulty suggesting evaluation questions, so the evaluator generated a list of proposed evaluation questions and then facilitated a discussion with the program staff. This helped program staff to begin suggesting their own ideas about ways to improve the list of questions, and some of the staff even added their own questions to the list.

At the outset, the goal is to capture all of the important evaluation questions. It is better to generate too many evaluation questions than too few. Additionally, the list of evaluation questions should be shared with all of the different groups who will be affected by the evaluation. These program stakeholders are important sources of information about the evaluation, and consulting with them about the evaluation questions can prove valuable.

For the Mentoring Project, after the evaluator and the program staff completed the list of evaluation questions, board members reviewed the list. Additionally, a group of mentors and groups of program participants also were asked to comment on and add to the list of evaluation questions. Sharing evaluation questions allows the emergence of important areas of the program in need of evaluation.

Questions were grouped together when they focused on similar aspects of the program. For the Mentoring Project, questions clustered into three areas: (a) mentor recruitment and training, (b) scope of activities, and (c) effects of the program on mentors and youth. Evaluation questions should be broad enough to allow for different sources of information to be used but not so broad as to allow the evaluation to roam aimlessly. For example, "How effective was the Mentoring Project?" is much too broad a question. The term *effective* means many different things to different people. Rather, "To what extent do youth participants succeed academically?" relays much more definition about the area to be investigated. Of course, each of the evaluation questions can be broken down into more specific questions, but this activity is better left until the proposal has been accepted and the evaluation commissioned.

SELECTING AN EVALUATION DESIGN

Once the evaluator has grouped and identified the most important evaluation questions, it is important to reflect on what type of evaluation will be most useful to the program. Thinking about the evaluation design usually causes the evaluator to expand the list of evaluation questions and shapes the direction of the evaluation. In selecting the evaluation design, the evaluator must consider five essential elements:

1. What is the balance needed between evaluating program outcomes (summative evaluation) versus evaluating ways to improve the program (formative evaluation)?

2. Which evaluation approaches, as described in Chapter 1 (i.e., objectives, management, consumer, expertise, adversary, and participant), will best suit the evaluation purpose?

3. Who are the primary audiences for the evaluation? Who will find the results interesting and who will use them?

4. Which parts of the evaluation are best guided by internal evaluators and which are best left to external evaluators?

5. Will comparative data be available to include for important outcomes?

Formative Versus Summative Evaluation

Evaluation for program improvement, formative evaluation, is almost always useful. In the beginning of a program, formative evaluation suggests and supports program adjustments that will result in better services. Toward the end of a program, when the emphasis is usually on outcome attainment, formative information can promote understanding what a program did to achieve the outcomes, which is as important as knowing the extent to which the outcomes were achieved.

Evaluation to determine program accomplishments, summative evaluation, is very important. Most people associated with social service programs consider their program of paramount importance. They want to know if the program has made a difference. Demonstrating the achievement of desired outcomes, however, can be problematic. If the goals of a program are lofty and broad, such as improving the quality of life for children under 6 years old and their families, then demonstrating an effect could take a long time. Even if a positive effect is observable, as time passes, factors beyond the program also influence change, and it becomes harder to draw definitive conclusions about the program's contribution to the desired outcome. Another problem with summative evaluation is that people often harbor unrealistic expectations about what a program can accomplish in a given time period. Programs just beginning implementation are unlikely to achieve major outcomes in the first year of operation. Similarly, a program like the Mentoring Project, in which mentors meet weekly for an hour with students, is unlikely to have a major effect on standardized achievement test scores, as the time allocated by the program is just too short to expect a major effect.

Another concern related to summative evaluation is tracking the degree and type of program implementation, particularly with multisite programs. Different sites will most likely implement the same program differently. Suppose a program shows no overall effect but at five of the 15 sites, positive outcomes are observed. It is unfair to say the program has no effect when formative data show that the five demonstrating improvement were the only five to implement the program in its entirety.

SELECTING EVALUATION APPROACHES

Considering different evaluation approaches can prove useful because evaluation purposes differ greatly. To review some of the material introduced in chapter 1, the most commonly used approaches include objective oriented, decision making, consumer oriented, and descriptive. The objective-oriented approach considers the extent to which program objectives have been achieved. The decision-making approach provides information needed by program administrators to determine future program directions. The consumer-oriented approach considers the effects of the program on stakeholders (e.g., participants, staff, community). The descriptive approach chronicles the important aspects of program implementation for public judgment. Often evaluators use multiple approaches tailored to fit the evaluation purpose.

Many people equate program evaluation with the objective-oriented approach, but this can be limiting to an evaluator. Program objectives are always important but may or may not be relevant to a specific evaluation purpose. A program might be too new to consider whether the goals have been achieved, or the evaluation might be commissioned expressly to measure client satisfaction, which may have nothing directly to do with achieving the program's objectives.

AUDIENCE

The groups interested in the evaluation results should be considered when designing the evaluation. Boards of directors are usually interested in different types of information than technically competent program personnel. The type of information released to the public is usually different from that released to a technical panel. The evaluator must consider the audiences for the evaluation and plan carefully so that the information available will effectively meet diverse needs.

INTERNAL VERSUS EXTERNAL EVALUATORS

Internal evaluators (evaluators who work directly for the program) are usually familiar with the program. External evaluators are engaged from outside the program, usually have limited knowledge about it, and thereby bring a fresh eye to the observation of program events. By virtue of the place of employment, internal evaluators are more available to program staff than external evaluators; also, they will be there to provide evaluation assistance after the external evaluator leaves. External evaluators are more likely to gather and report sensitive information about a program because their livelihood is not entirely dependent on the program. Furthermore, people usually feel more confident sharing negative feedback about a program with someone who does not have a vested interest in its outcomes. External evaluators can lend credibility to a program evaluation in two important ways: (a) they have reputations that extend beyond the program that lend weight to their findings; and (b) they are familiar with other, similar programs and can draw useful comparisons. In planning the evaluation, the client and evaluator must consider the strengths and weaknesses of both types of evaluators and make recommendations accordingly.

COMPARATIVE DATA POSSIBILITIES

When considering important program outcomes, the availability of comparative data is fundamental to many evaluations. This is especially important in today's federal program environment, which places heavy emphasis on research-based results. In an ideally controlled environment, such as that of a greenhouse, random selection and assignment to treatment and control groups will yield exceptionally strong support for any effects of the treatment. But life, and particularly life in schools or social programs, rarely allows for such controls. Equivalent comparison groups can be useful (Smith & Glass, 1987), but serious caution is warranted in deciding whether the comparison group is actually equivalent to the treatment group. Another alternative is making comparisons of the participants in the program with similar school district, county, state, or national comparison groups. Still another strategy is to conduct pre- and posttests that compare where students began and where they end. Much has been written about experimental and quasiexperimental design (see, for example, Campbell & Stanley, 1966, or Cook & Campbell, 1979, for a thorough discussion). The evaluator needs to explore comparison group options when designing the evaluation.

Matching Information-Gathering Options With Evaluation Questions

After evaluation questions are drafted, with assistance from the various program stakeholders, and the evaluation design is considered, the evaluator must identify the types of information needed and how that information will be collected. At this juncture, consultation with the client is important, but useful feedback can be difficult to obtain because most clients lack adequate evaluation experience.

Constructing an "evaluation crosswalk" (O'Sullivan, 1991) can facilitate this step of the evaluation. The evaluation crosswalk is a technique for demonstrating to clients how evaluation questions are linked to data collection strategies. Through the development of an evaluation crosswalk, evaluators create a matrix that shows how each evaluation question is linked to proposed information-gathering techniques. In this manner, clients may see how proposed data collection procedures will be used to answer various evaluation questions, and evaluators can ensure adequate triangulation of data sources. Triangulation is the process of using more than one data source to verify findings; replication of findings across multiple sources gives credence to statements and judgments. The evaluation crosswalk is an activity that helps to focus the evaluation proposal and later can be used to monitor implementation of the evaluation.

For example, when an evaluator tells a client that focus groups are planned for the evaluation, most clients hear the technical side of the communication and assume that their input is unnecessary. Focus groups are what evaluators do, and most clients will say little about the selected data collection technique. Evaluation crosswalks encourage clients to scrutinize the feasibility of the selected techniques. Clients realize that they can have a say in the data collection process and may make useful suggestions.

Using an evaluation crosswalk with the Mentoring Project, the evaluator told the client that a focus group would be used to find out from participants how they viewed the program and the extent to which their mentorship worked. When the client considered this data collection strategy in the context of the evaluation questions, its advisability was thought to be questionable. The client knew that Mentoring Project participants had never been brought together before and that, as a rule, at-risk students do not interact well in formal groups with their peers. This information allowed the evaluator to modify the evaluation plan so that Mentoring Project participants would be individually interviewed rather than asked to participate in a focus group. Without the evaluation crosswalk, the evaluator could have seriously misstepped, causing delays in the evaluation. With the evaluation crosswalk, clients can actively participate in the data collection planning process.

EVALUATION CROSSWALK FOR THE RURAL ECONOMIC DEVELOPMENT PROGRAM

Figure 4.4 shows the evaluation crosswalk for the Rural Economic Development Program. The important program components to be evaluated

Rural Health and Economic Development Program

Data Sources

1 = Funding and refunding applications
2 = Site visit reports and foundation documents
3 = Grantees' internal evaluation documents
4 = Focus groups of grantee boards and staff
5 = Annual survey of grantees
6 = Case studies

Evaluation Questions	1	2	3	4	5	6
I. Enhanced health and economic development						
1. To what extent have projects promoted rural health and/or economic development?	X	X	X	X		X
2. How have rural communities benefited from project activities?	X	X	X	X		X
3. In what ways should the foundation modify its support of rural economic development?		X			X	
II. Strengthened infrastructure						
1. To what extent are projects using evaluation as a tool for keeping their activities effective?	X	X	X			
2. How have projects strengthened the capacity of rural communities?	X	X				X
III. Collaborative Work						
1. In what ways have grantees enhanced existing organizational and personal networks?		X			X	X
2. How has enhanced networking promoted rural health and economic development?	X	X	X	X		
3. In what ways should the foundation modify its support of collaborative work?		X			X	

Figure 4.4   Evaluation Crosswalk

were identified, and the questions were grouped into logical clusters and organized hierarchically. Evaluation questions were then generated for each component. Notice that the questions are broad in scope: They are probing, open-ended–type questions rather than questions that can be answered yes or no. Notice also that the evaluation questions use multiple data collection strategies to arrive at the responses to a particular question. Generally, information from multiple data sources paints a clearer picture of the program and provides more persuasive evidence of program accomplishments and events than information from a single source. Finally, notice that the evaluation data collection procedures include the use of existing documents and information regularly collected by the program. Program documents can provide strong foundations on which to build evaluative evidence. In most cases, the evaluator will rely on existing program documentation as an important data source.

The evaluator should include an explanation of each proposed data collection strategy in the evaluation proposal narrative, paying special attention to those strategies that might not be well known to the client. The evaluator also should identify who will be asked to provide information and how people will be selected to provide evaluation information. Additionally, the evaluator will need to assign responsibilities for collecting the information.

In addition to eliciting important feedback from the program, the evaluation crosswalk also can be used by the evaluator to develop evaluation instruments. At the point where the focus group protocol for the meetings with project staff must be developed, the evaluator can review the evaluation crosswalk to verify that all necessary questions are included. Additionally, questions proposed for the focus group protocol but unrelated to the crosswalk should be omitted.

Listing Important Evaluation Activities

The next section of the evaluation proposal contains a list of important evaluation activities. The purpose of the list is to provide the client with a clear idea of what will occur during the evaluation and when. The list is usually organized as a timeline, showing the sequence of evaluation events. Depending on the duration of the evaluation, the timeline may be organized by years, months, or weeks.

Figure 4.5 shows a timeline of important activities in the evaluation of the Mentoring Project. Essential evaluation activities are listed by month. The amount of time it will take to draft instruments and pilot test them are important considerations. Collecting information, analyzing collected data, writing draft reports, and having program personnel review the drafts are other essentials that are frequently overlooked but take significant amounts of time.

Mentoring Project Evaluation Timeline

Month 1	Develop expanded evaluation plan with Mentoring Project staff
	Review and augment timeline with Mentoring Project staff
	Review project documents
Month 2	Draft and pilot test mentor focus group protocol
	Draft and pilot test participants' telephone interviews
	Identify samples for focus groups and telephone interviews
Month 3	Conduct focus groups with mentors
	Summarize project document data
	Meet with staff to review evaluation progress
	Summarize focus group data and return to participants for review
	Begin telephone interviews with participants
Month 4	Analyze mentor focus group data
	Complete telephone interviews with participants
Month 5	Analyze participant telephone interview data
	Draft final report and send to Mentoring Project for review
Month 6	Modify evaluation report as needed
	Present evaluation report to Mentoring Project board and staff

Figure 4.5   Evaluation Timeline

For more complicated evaluation, a program evaluation and review technique (PERT) chart may be more useful. Figure 4.6 shows the evaluation activities for the Rural Economic Development Program placed in a PERT chart. One advantage of PERT charts over timelines is that they show the flow of each activity over time. If the evaluation has a number of components, the activities associated with the component can be easily traced with a PERT chart. For example, in the evaluation of the Rural Economic Development Program, the case study component can be traced from beginning to end, making it easier to see how activities are related. Particularly for complex evaluations, PERT charts allow the evaluation activities to be broken into their various components, with a timeline constructed for each.

Rural Economic Development Program Evaluation Timeline

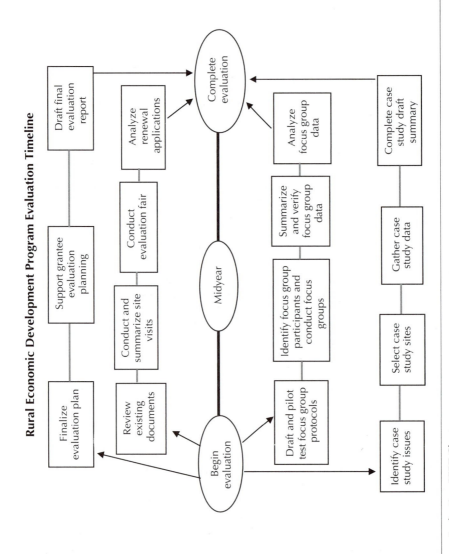

Figure 4.6   Evaluation PERT Chart

Summarizing Personnel and Organization Qualifications

An important part of the evaluation proposal is for the evaluator to communicate to the client both the qualifications of personnel who will be involved with the evaluation and the organizational resources that will be available for conducting the evaluation. Usually, complete resumes of key evaluation personnel are appended to the proposal. Within the proposal, however, a section should summarize and highlight the information in the resumes that is most germane to the evaluation. Experience with similar program evaluations is usually something that clients view positively. Previous reports or publications relevant to the evaluation, as well as specialized knowledge of the program, also are assets.

Organizational resources include both direct support available for the evaluation and indirect support that can be called on if needed. Examples of direct support include clerical staff, fax and e-mail capability, and computing facilities. Indirect support can include library resources, community resources, support networks, professional organizations, and graduate students. The proposal is trying to give the client some sense of what resources the evaluator brings to the evaluation.

In this section, the evaluator may also include a summary of previous evaluations that have been completed. This summary also may include names and addresses of references that the client may contact for information about the evaluator's work. Occasionally, the client asks for copies of previous evaluation reports; these may be appended to the proposal.

Budgeting

Estimating the budget for the evaluation is an extremely important activity for both the client and the evaluator. Not only do clients want to know where their resources will be spent; the evaluator wants to make sure that the resources available will support the proposed evaluation. If the evaluator promises an evaluation that is underbudgeted, the results are usually disastrous. Either the evaluator is forced to tell the client that the evaluation cannot proceed due to lack of funds, or the evaluator goes ahead and completes the evaluation but has to absorb the additional costs. Neither alternative makes for good evaluation. Rather, the evaluator should make every effort to realistically estimate the cost of the evaluation.

How much an evaluation should cost is relative to the size of the program and the purpose of the evaluation. Size is important, because evaluation resources come from program management funds, and smaller programs usually have fewer funds and proportionally fewer management resources than larger programs. For example, a small program with a total budget of less than $50,000 probably could not afford to allocate 10% of its budget to evaluation. Even if it did, $5,000 would probably not be enough to purchase adequate evaluation assistance. On the other hand, a $2 million project might have 10% to allocate to evaluation but would probably not need a $200,000 design. Of course, when the evaluation findings will be used to make important decisions about the program, higher investments are warranted.

A number of budgeting formats are available to assist the evaluator in this endeavor. For people just starting out, more detail is better than less. Creating a budget always begins with the list of important activities, which the evaluator uses to estimate costs. Some clients have a preferred budget format that should be used in the proposal. Some formats require a budget narrative, in which the evaluator explains what is included in a certain budget item and how certain costs were estimated.

Figure 4.7 shows the budget worksheet for the Mentoring Project. The timeline of important activities has been transferred to a budget sheet that includes personnel time, travel, and other budgetary resources items. The evaluator determines who will be involved in each activity, estimates how much time that activity will take, and anticipates additional resources needed.

After establishing personnel rates of pay, time commitments, travel projections, and other necessary expenditures, budget calculations can proceed. Information from the worksheet (Figure 4.7) is then transferred to the budget summary page (see Figure 4.8). Added to the budget are estimates of general office supplies, general copying expenses, postage, telephone, and so on. For the Mentoring Project, personnel are working as consultants and are paid at a per diem rate. With evaluations that employ people and pay them based on a percentage of an annual salary, fringe benefits to the employees also must be included. Indirect costs, also known as overhead, include costs incurred by the evaluator for general operation of the project, such as office space, office furniture, and utilities. When large organizations such as universities bid on evaluation contracts, the indirect costs rate is usually fixed as a percentage of personnel costs. Some for-profit consulting firms also have established indirect cost rates. The budget worksheet is usually included in the proposal only when an itemized budget narrative is requested.

For the Mentoring Project budget presented, personnel required the greatest amount of the budgetary resources. This is common with evaluation budgets. Because personnel are the major expenditure, one way to keep costs competitive is to plan the evaluation with different levels of support personnel. For example, the evaluation assistant is paid at a lower rate than the evaluator; therefore the evaluation assistant should perform as many tasks as possible rather than having the evaluator perform tasks that could be paid at a lower rate.

Mentoring Project Budget

Evaluation Activities	Resources Needed	Amount (in US$)
• Develop expanded evaluation plan with staff • Review and augment timeline with staff	Evaluator, 2 days Travel to project (1 day @ $75/day, 150 miles round trip @ $.31/mile)	1000 75 47
• Review project documents	Evaluation assistant, 5 days	1000
• Draft and pilot test mentor focus group protocol	Evaluator, 2 days Evaluation assistant, 6 days	1000 1200
• Draft and pilot test participants' telephone interviews	Evaluator, 2 days Evaluation assistant, 6 days	1000 1200
• Identify samples for focus groups and telephone interviews	Evaluation assistant, 5 days	1000
• Conduct focus groups with mentors	Evaluator, 2 days Evaluation assistant, 6 days	1000 1200
• Summarize project document data	Evaluation assistant, 10 days	2000
• Meet with staff to review evaluation progress	Evaluator, ½ day Travel to project (1 day @ $75/day, 150 miles round trip @ $.31/mile)	250 75 47
• Summarize focus group data and return to participants for review	Evaluation assistant, 5 days	1000
• Begin telephone interviews with participants	Evaluation assistant, 5 days Telephone (150 calls @ $2/call)	1000 300
• Analyze mentor focus group data	Evaluation assistant, 4 days	800
• Complete telephone interviews with participants	Evaluation assistant, 4 days Telephone (75 calls @ $2/call)	800 150
• Analyze participant telephone interview data	Evaluator, 1 day Evaluation assistant (5 days)	500 1000
• Draft final report and send to staff for review	Evaluator, 4 days	2000
• Modify evaluation report as needed	Evaluator, 1 day Printing 20 copies @ $5/copy	500 100
• Present evaluation report to board and staff	Evaluator, ½ day Travel to project (1 day @ $75/day, 150 miles round trip @ $.31/mile)	250 75 47

Figure 4.7   Evaluation Budget Worksheet

Mentoring Project Budget

		Cost of Personnel (in US$)
	Evaluator (15 days @ $500/day)	7500
	Evaluation assistant (63 days @ $200/day)	12,600
Travel:		
	(3 days @ $75/day lodging + meals)	225
	(3 trips @ 150 miles × $.31/mile)	140
Communication:		
	General telephone	200
	Telephone surveys (225 calls @ $2/call)	450
Copies:		
	General	200
	Final report (20 copies @ $5/copy)	
Supplies:		500
Total direct costs		21,815
Indirect costs (overhead @ 10% total direct)		2182
Total evaluation costs		23,997

Figure 4.8   Evaluation Budget Summary

Presentation of the Proposal

The previous eight elements of an evaluation proposal combine and culminate in its presentation to the client. Although some of the elements of the proposal directly support collaborative evaluation goals (e.g., the evaluation crosswalk), timelines, personnel qualifications, and budgets are common to most proposals. What sets the collaborative evaluation stance apart is the importance placed on communication with the client and other stakeholders. Presentation of the proposal is important for ensuring a successful collaborative response to an evaluation request.

In general, the language of the proposal should be clear and as free of jargon as possible. Check to correct any typographic, spelling, and grammatical errors. The graphic presentation of the proposal should be inviting, well laid out, and easy to read, with as few distractions as possible.

A number of strategies will assist in promoting language clarity and avoiding jargon. The most powerful strategy is to have the proposal proofread. Different people can perform different proofreading services. People similar to the client or funder but with limited evaluation background can read the proposal to make sure the language is clear and free of evaluation jargon. People unfamiliar with the program can help in determining if the language is free of programmatic jargon. Proofreading by other evaluators also will assist with this, as well as verifying the soundness of the evaluation approach.

In today's world of word processors and desktop publishing capabilities, evaluators are able to avail themselves of the latest technology and produce evaluation proposals that are incredibly well designed and that can be presented in an inviting (and even colorful) manner. Most people prefer pictures to words; therefore, tables, charts, figures, and illustrations facilitate the communication process. For example, many people find that the evaluation crosswalk helps them conceptualize the entire evaluation; something they have difficulty doing with only an expanded narrative.

Occasionally, evaluators will have the opportunity to make a formal presentation of the proposal to the funder. In this instance, the evaluator needs to provide a brief overview of the evaluation and should assume that the funders will have questions about the proposal that need answering. Often these questions focus on terms unfamiliar to the funder or ask for more detail about a particular proposed evaluation strategy. As an alternative to a formal presentation, the client may ask the evaluator to respond in writing to questions raised by the proposal reviewers. In this case, the rules of good proposal writing are still in effect: (a) clear and jargon-free writing that is (b) grammatically correct without spelling or typing errors and (c) graphically inviting.

Summary of Chapter Contents

This chapter presented the elements of a collaborative evaluation proposal, which extended the clarification process of chapter 3 to the next level. Together, inclusion of the program background statement, evaluation purpose, evaluation crosswalk, timeline, qualifications statement, and budget, all of which culminate in a presentation of the proposal to the client, will promote a collaborative evaluation stance. The majority of evaluation proposals will contain similar elements, but collaborative evaluation proposals emphasize the importance of engaging the client and stakeholders in proposal development. The key is in promoting communication concerning the proposal. The chapter briefly explains each element and, where useful, provides examples. The elements provide prospective clients with information that allows them to knowledgeably decide on a course of action for their evaluation.

Chapter 4 Exercises

TEFLEP EVALUATION

Recall from the previous chapter's exercises that the TEFLEP project created a 3-year, youth advocacy and support program intended to (a) reduce infant morbidity and mortality by convincing mothers to use government-sponsored maternal and child healthcare clinics, (b) improve job prospects among participants by encouraging them to return to school or aiding them in securing employment, (c) increase father-child bonding by encouraging fathers to provide greater economic and emotional support to their children, and (d) reduce incidences of second pregnancy by providing family planning education and supplies to both mothers and fathers.

The evaluation design had the 151 program participants and the 35 control group teens complete enrollment, postpartum, and 6-, 12-, 18-, and 24-month follow-up interviews. During the interviews, teens were asked about their babies' health, their educational and employment activities, their contact with the fathers, and their family planning activities, including new pregnancies. The only other available data about the project was a set of included project progress reports sent to the ministry and the funding agency.

By the end of the 3-year project, all but 3 of the 151 participants were active to some degree, but only 18 of the 35 controls were willing to continue their participation. Preliminary data indicated that there were 36 second pregnancies among participants and 7 second pregnancies among the controls.

Activity

Think through how you can improve the evaluation design. What are the important evaluation questions? Can the currently available data answer these important evaluation questions? What, if any, additional data sources do you think would strengthen the evaluation?

5

Collaborative
Evaluation Techniques

Collaborative evaluation mirrors much of the general field of evaluation with similar strategies and practices, but some techniques are unique to it. In the previous chapter, which discussed how to design a collaborative evaluation, the nine elements identified for developing an evaluation proposal were common to most other evaluation approaches; the six described for collaborative evaluation built on the initial clarification activity and mandated inclusion of stakeholders in the proposal development stage. Most evaluation proposals contain an evaluation design, evaluation questions, timeline, budget, and so on. For the most part, what separates collaborative evaluation from other approaches is not those activities but how those activities are conducted. At each juncture of clarification and proposal development, feedback loops are created so that collaboration begins even before the evaluation starts.

Four activities do stand out as decidedly collaborative in nature and are not likely to be part of more traditional evaluation practices: collaborative evaluation planning, evaluation fairs, evaluation technical assistance, and evaluation capacity building.

This chapter describes these four activities in detail and uses the three examples—the Mentoring Project, the Rural Economic Development Program, and Volunteers Across America—to further demonstrate how they can be used in different evaluation contexts.

Collaborative Evaluation Planning

Collaborative evaluations that interface with internal evaluators, multiple projects or programs, or multiple sites often must coordinate evaluation efforts among these groups. This also is true when sponsoring organization staff share responsibility for monitoring program progress or grantee accountability. In addition, with limited external evaluation budgets, program staff may become important members of the external evaluation team by collecting, analyzing, and reporting portions of evaluation data needed to answer the evaluation questions.

INTERFACING WITH OTHER EVALUATION EFFORTS

When a collaborative evaluation is designed and commissioned, the evaluator needs to make sure that the proposed efforts are integrated with others that are planned. If an external collaborative evaluator is conducting the evaluation, internal evaluation plans must be identified. Multiple projects and multiple sites compound the endeavor's complexity; this is true whether the evaluator is internal or external.

For example, evaluation is multilevel with Volunteers Across America (VAA), the federally funded, national education project that involves 250 program sites across the United States. The sponsoring federal agency requires programs to assess project outcomes and to provide information to enable the agency to monitor program activities for project renewal purposes. Some of the VAA projects are administered by state or local government agencies that also have their own evaluation requirements. In addition, many of the projects collect information of interest to them about program services but that is not required by either the federal or the parent agency. The external evaluation proposed for VAA must work within this context and schedule external evaluation activities around these other evaluation requirements. Where possible, data collection efforts need to be streamlined and duplication of effort avoided.

PROGRAM STAFF AND MONITORING

Usually, program evaluators are not asked to monitor program progress for accountability purposes. Monitoring involves making sure that program funds are spent in a manner consistent with proposed activities. Usually, depending on the size and the organization of a program, clerical, contract, financial, administrative, or program staff gather information that allows them to judge whether a program is meeting its primary obligations. Thus, staff members follow the day-to-day operations of a program, usually through regular (e.g., monthly, quarterly) reports that contain financial and service statistics. Auditors, not program evaluators, normally would be the group called in to verify these records. Program evaluators, although not directly involved in program monitoring, should acquaint themselves with monitoring requirements so that they may coordinate program evaluation schedules with monitoring schedules.

The Mentoring Project Example

With the Mentoring Project, initially the director of the program wanted someone to help with the monitoring aspects of the project. She wanted to know how many volunteer mentors they had placed, the amount and type of training the volunteers received, and how many of the program participants attended the program. Until the external evaluator met with the director and the program staff, very little record keeping was being done. The program staff told the evaluator that they knew the program was successful because of the high demand for program assistance. They had opted, therefore, to spend time delivering services rather than keeping records. The evaluator needed to build the external evaluation, in part, on the monitoring information and so worked with program staff to devise a record-keeping system they both could use. Program staff agreed to collect and summarize the monitoring information. The evaluator helped them set up a database on their computer for that purpose. If the evaluator had not consulted with the project staff about monitoring activities, a serious problem would have arisen when project statistics were needed for the outcome evaluation that had been commissioned.

EXPANDING EVALUATION TEAMS WITH PROGRAM STAFF

Often programs have inadequate resources to engage external evaluators in pursuit of the answers to pressing evaluation questions. A collaborative evaluator can find ways to structure the evaluation such that program staff can join the evaluation team and assist with providing the desired information. This is especially true with large multisite programs in which the number of programs and the travel distance would increase external evaluation costs appreciably.

Collaborative evaluators can enlist the assistance of key program staff in designing evaluations for their efforts that will contribute to the overall program evaluation. Assuming different program components or sites, the staff of each component or site can be recruited to develop and implement an evaluation plan for their particular program processes and outcomes. As each component or site is responsible for its evaluation, the external or internal evaluator can concentrate on continuity across programs and cross-site data gathering and analyses.

In this situation, collaborative evaluators train program staff to become evaluators, as they would any other evaluation team member. Skills among program staff, now program evaluation team members, may vary greatly.

Happily, many will bring an appreciable amount of understanding, expertise, and even enthusiasm to the endeavor; others will require more training and support. The collaborative evaluator assesses the program evaluation skills of the staff, divides the tasks in consultation with them, and then provides support and assistance where needed to help them complete assigned tasks.

Developing this layered, collaborative evaluation approach has a number of potential advantages. Evaluation efforts are expanded, program staff are more aware of evaluation plans and practices, evaluation questions better reflect program needs, evaluators garner more cooperation in cross-site or-component evaluation efforts, the quality of the data gathered and reported improves, and use of evaluation findings increases.

In implementing this approach, the collaborative evaluator needs to think carefully about the time demands that program evaluation may place on program staff. For this strategy to work, program staff must be collaboratively engaged in deciding both what needs to be done and what roles they might assume. Together with the collaborative evaluator, realistic responsibilities can be carved from what needs to occur.

This collaborative approach promotes expanded evaluation efforts in that component- or site-level data are now available as well as cross-site data. Had the evaluation not included program staff, the limited evaluation resources would not have stretched to collect all the information desired. Further, the costs associated with collecting component- or site-level information for an external evaluator are greater than for program staff.

As program staff members plan their component or site evaluations, they become more aware of evaluation plans and practices. This awareness can extend to the overall program evaluation design. As staff better understand the scope and sequence of evaluation, the evaluation questions can be amended to better reflect program needs. Further, with program staff considered members of the same team, evaluators garner more cooperation in cross-site and component evaluation efforts. Rather than being external to the program component or site, the evaluator is now seen as a coworker who is more likely to elicit cooperation than not. As members of the evaluation team, staff also better understand the purposes of data collection and reporting and thus the quality improves. Finally, the more program personnel understand and value evaluation as members of the expanded evaluation team, the more utilization of evaluation findings is likely to increase.

The Rural Economic Development Program Example

The Rural Economic Development Program provides an example of how collaborative evaluation can engage program staff in a way that expands the evaluation team, thereby extending the comprehensiveness of overall evaluation efforts. In the first year of the program, ten communities had been granted funding for a number of different projects in each community, all aimed at promoting rural health and economic development. Even though the external evaluator proposed to visit each of the sites once a year, an annual visit of a few days did not permit sufficient opportunity to directly evaluate either process or outcome aspects of the individual projects in each of the communities.

The evaluator proposed that each of the ten community project coordinators meet to develop evaluation plans for each of their sites. The evaluator facilitated this meeting and shared a logic model format with the project coordinators to promote common evaluation planning. That logic model format, shown in Figure 5.1, asked grantees to integrate project objectives with activities, identify the program outcomes that would occur as a result of the activities, and then show the types of evidence that would be used to measure those results.

Coordinators were asked to return to their sites and discuss evaluation needs within their project and draft evaluation plans. The project coordinators were instructed to send the draft plans to the evaluator for comment in the next 3 weeks and were encouraged to contact the evaluator if they needed clarification or assistance. During the 3-week period, three of the project coordinators called with questions, one faxed a draft to the evaluator for comment, and one sent a draft attachment by e-mail. By the 3-week deadline, all but two of the ten plans had arrived, and the evaluator contacted the two project coordinators who had not sent in their drafts to see what, if any, assistance was needed in completing the plans. The evaluator reviewed all eight plans that were sent, making minor comments on four, suggesting major changes on three, and calling one coordinator for clarification as the plan sent made little sense. A week later, the two outstanding plans arrived; one needed only minor adjustments, and the second required a number of e-mail exchanges and a conference call. The plan that had made little sense arrived in a much improved second-draft form.

During this planning phase, the evaluator was careful not to take over the planning process. As projects struggle with evaluation planning, evaluators can be tempted to write the plan for struggling projects or to make the corrections. When that occurs, however, the projects may distance themselves from the process and allow the plan to become the evaluator's. This diminishes the likelihood that the project will take the responsibility necessary to implement the evaluation.

This evaluation planning set the stage to engage the ten project sites in evaluating their individual project efforts. Projects now had plans that they had developed and revised. Through this process, the evaluator was aware of what the programs hoped to accomplish and also knew firsthand the evaluation expertise within the program.

Program Objectives	Activities	Outcomes	Evidence Used to Measure Outcomes
Objective 1			
Objective 2			
Objective 3			

Figure 5.1   Logic Model for Evaluation Planning

Evaluation Fairs, Conferences, and Showcases

The presence of an evaluation plan does not guarantee that the plan will be implemented. Initially, evaluation plans can be treated as just another meaningless hoop that programs need to jump through to receive funding for services but intend to jettison as soon as possible. Just as grant writers view the evaluation section in project proposals as hollow, at the outset of collaborative evaluation planning, programs will usually comply with the requirements—but often in the hope that they will not have to implement their plans. Sometimes competing time commitments make it very difficult for program staff to meet deadlines. When that happens, collaborative evaluators must work with program staff to assist them. This might be done over the phone or via e-mail, or a meeting may need to be scheduled so that evaluators and staff can work on the plan together.

An event at which programs can share their evaluation results is not only a very powerful networking tool for multisite component programs; it also reinforces the value of implementing the evaluation plan. These events have been called evaluation fairs, evaluation conferences, and program showcases (O'Sullivan, 1999a; O'Sullivan & D'Agostino, 1998, 2002), and they can provide opportunities for networking and reinforcement. Basically, evaluation fairs bring programs together to share their evaluation findings. At the evaluation planning stage, the evaluator explains that the evaluation plans will be used to implement the evaluation, the results of which will be shared at the evaluation fair. Initially, sharing is done among peers to reduce the anxiety that surrounds evaluation and a new experience. Later, as people become accustomed to the fair, other stakeholders may be invited to the event. The sharing can be a short presentation or a poster session and may include handouts. Usually, the programs receive a written explanation of the fair format and an outline of what should be covered during the presentation. The evaluation fair may be taped to share with others and to summarize accomplishments across the programs.

The Rural Economic Development Program's Evaluation Fair

The ten projects in the Rural Economic Development Program completed their evaluation plans and were told that at midyear they would be asked to come to an evaluation fair and present their evaluation findings to date. Projects were encouraged to bring three people to the fair. The evaluator wanted this date to be earlier in the project year rather than later to encourage projects not to delay implementation of their evaluation plans. The evaluation fair also would be a way to identify projects that were struggling with implementation, thereby allowing time for technical assistance before the end of the first project year.

Many projects welcomed this opportunity to network and find out what other projects were doing. Some liked the idea but were concerned about what was required and who needed to attend. The evaluator offered all ten projects assistance in getting ready for the fair and assured those that expressed some anxiety that only project personnel were invited to attend this first fair. Representatives of the foundation funding the program and community groups would be invited to subsequent evaluation fairs.

The evaluator received assistance requests from three of the ten projects. One request was from a project coordinator who was developing her first PowerPoint presentation and had some questions. Another asked the evaluator to review a participant satisfaction survey that the project was developing. The third request was from a project coordinator who really wanted someone to visit and explain what needed to happen to get ready for the evaluation fair. The evaluator was able to comply with this request as part of an already scheduled site visit.

As the fair was the first event at which projects met together, the agenda for the day included presentations about each program that were aided by table displays. The presentation and displays contained information about program intents, components, partners, and activities. This 2-hour session (each project had 10 minutes to present) was followed by a 90-minute luncheon, an informal networking session during which people were free to contact fellow participants and talk. After lunch, 2 hours were set aside again for programs to share their evaluation results. If sufficient time had not elapsed for the project to arrive at evaluation results, project coordinators shared information about their evaluation instruments. The two projects that had experienced delays in starting program activities, which in turn delayed implementing the evaluation, shared their evaluation plans.

The evaluator made sure that participants had the opportunity to evaluate their evaluation fair experience. All 30 participants rated the opportunity the fair provided to share among themselves as "Excellent" on the evaluation form. Responses to open-ended questions on the form expressed participants' desire to continue this type of activity and generally expressed the positive nature of coming together to share accomplishments. In addition, participants identified evaluation topics for future exploration as well as requesting assistance from the evaluator.

The evaluator summarized the information from the evaluation fair to create a description of each of the projects and what they had done to date. Each description was sent back to its project for approval prior to the evaluator's compiling all the descriptions and distributing the compilation to the participants and the foundation.

Evaluation Technical Assistance

At each juncture of the collaborative evaluation activities—evaluation planning, implementation, and evaluation fair—the evaluator should offer assistance in completing the necessary tasks. This type of evaluation technical assistance allows program staff who are inexperienced with evaluation to progressively enhance their competence in evaluation. Over time, this enhanced competence translates into evaluation efforts that increase in quality and thus worth to the program.

This technical assistance can take many forms and occurs at different levels. Usually with multisite or multicomponent programs, the need for technical assistance varies such that the evaluator is not inundated with requests. Depending on the evaluation readiness of the person requesting assistance, the help could range from minor reassurances via voice or e-mail about the correctness of a particular evaluation task to multiple, in-depth, face-to-face visits. The person requesting or receiving the assistance could be someone well versed in evaluation and enthusiastic about the activity or someone who is virtually clueless about evaluation and resents not being allowed to keep it that way. The evaluator's job is to recognize the type of technical assistance needed and the collaboration level desired.

Another responsibility of the collaborative evaluator is to recognize the various needs for technical assistance and the importance of taking proactive action to provide assistance. Often program people will not recognize their need, are reluctant to request assistance, or would just prefer not to spend the time required to complete the evaluation task. The evaluator must anticipate these situations and respond accordingly. This is why, in the examples, both with collaborative evaluation planning and the evaluation fair, the events were structured so that the evaluator could triage program needs for technical assistance.

Evaluation technical assistance as part of a collaborative evaluation approach is more than evaluation consulting. In the collaborative evaluation context, program staff members are part of the evaluation team. With totally external, distanced evaluations, members of the evaluation team vary in their levels of evaluation expertise. More often than not, evaluation assistants ask senior evaluators to review instruments that they develop. They also might ask for advice about sampling, pilot testing, or data analysis and reporting. If they understand what needs to be done, they do not require assistance. This is precisely the type of assistance evaluators give to program staff in collaborative evaluation activities.

Evaluation Capacity Building

Collaborative evaluation in and of itself usually results in the enhanced capacity of programs to conduct and commission evaluations, but separate evaluation capacity-building events are also part of the collaborative evaluation repertoire. These capacity-building activities range from formal, 5-day, introductory evaluation trainings to 1-hour, specific seminars focused on particular data collection or analysis techniques. Participants in the collaborative evaluation, the funders, or the evaluators can suggest evaluation capacity-building events.

Ultimately, the goal is to strengthen evaluation capacity within programs so that programs can assess their accomplishments and make improvements. Collaborative evaluators are in a uniquely advantageous position to facilitate this outcome. Not only are collaborative evaluators familiar with the program and the staff; they also understand the specific evaluation needs of the group. Within a single agency, an evaluator might provide training on how to use the database program that is being used to store program service statistics. For larger multicomponent or multisite programs, the collaborative evaluator can facilitate the sharing of instruments to measure specific outcomes, solicit suggestions for additional evaluation training and then orchestrate those events, or generate any number of other capacity-building activities.

Positive Outcomes of Collaborative Evaluation

The combination of evaluation planning, evaluation fairs, technical assistance, and capacity building has been shown to promote collaboration among programs, enhance evaluation understanding, and improve the quality of evaluation report writing (O'Sullivan & D'Agostino, 1998, 2002). Engaging program staff in evaluation planning, implementation, and reporting can expand evaluation efforts, increase program staff awareness of evaluation plans and practices, lead to evaluation questions that better reflect program needs, and promote cooperation in evaluation activities, thereby improving the quality of evaluation data. All of the positive outcomes ultimately should lead to better utilization of evaluation findings, because program staff have helped frame the evaluation from the beginning and have collaborated in the process. Thus they bring greater interest to the process and will be more likely to understand and act on findings.

The collaborative evaluator, whether internal or external to the program, assumes the stance of someone who works with program staff to answer evaluation questions about how well the program is working. Accompanying this stance is a belief that those engaged in the program genuinely want to know the degree to which program efforts have achieved the desired outcomes and how the program can improve. Thus, although it is not possible to shed bias completely, the collaborative evaluator can avoid that evaluation bias caused by lack of program understanding and distance from the evaluation context.

Summary of Chapter Contents

This chapter focused on four activities, included as part of collaborative evaluation, which decidedly engage stakeholders in evaluation. Collaborative evaluation planning brings stakeholders to the table such that evaluation activities are integrated within other program events. Evaluation fairs bring stakeholders together to share evaluation strategies and program accomplishments. Technical assistance provided in evaluation by the evaluator strengthens a program's ability to answer important evaluation questions. Finally, evaluation capacity building among program personnel enhances understanding about evaluation, promotes cooperation in evaluation activities, and enables programs to better manage their evaluation responsibilities.

6

Collaborative Data Gathering

L ike the other evaluation steps described in previous chapters, collaborative data gathering contains elements consistent with most other evaluation approaches, such as using evaluation questions to identify who will provide the information (sample selection) and selecting or developing instruments. The key difference with collaborative evaluation is how these activities are conducted. Collaborative evaluators seek out, during the planning stages of an evaluation, opportunities to engage stakeholders at each of these junctures. In this chapter, each of these topics is addressed, with special attention paid to how to conduct the activities collaboratively. Sample selection and instrument identification and development are explored.

The last section in this chapter uses the example of the Economic Rural Development Program evaluation to demonstrate how an evaluator might use a focus group to answer evaluation questions. The focus group was selected because it is a staple data collection strategy for evaluators.

Selecting Samples

USING THE EVALUATION CROSSWALK

The evaluation crosswalk developed with the evaluation plan provides an excellent guidebook from which to manage the evaluation. Assuming that the program staff have reviewed the data collection techniques proposed in the crosswalk and have agreed to them, the next step is to decide who will provide information for the various data collection strategies. Because the evaluation plan has been developed collaboratively, the likelihood of getting cooperation from those who have been identified as persons or agencies who will be providing information is greater than might be the case otherwise. Program staff can help evaluators identify strategies by which to select and encourage high participation rates among those from whom information is needed.

SAMPLING CHOICES

For every data collection activity, evaluators must identify the individuals who will provide the information. Specifying this sampling frame can be very easy or quite complicated. The evaluation purpose and the evaluation question, which create the need to collect information, will guide these choices. An evaluator might need to talk to all participants in a program (a census), a representative sample, or one or two individuals. This section discusses the advantages of different types of random sampling and purposive sampling to help guide future evaluation choices. For a more complete guide to quantitative sampling approaches, consult Henry (1990). For qualitative sampling strategies, consult Denzin and Lincoln (2000). The collaborative part comes in discussing options with program staff and together deciding on the best course of action.

Representativeness or Richness

Gathering information is a balance between needs and resources. The evaluator usually has limited resources with which to gather the evaluation information needed. The more people who are asked to provide information and the more information asked for, the more data there are to be analyzed and reported. Resources, which usually translate into some form of time, money, and pain, moderate sampling strategies. Given 300 program participants and a limited evaluation budget, the truism is that you can ask all 300 a few questions, a representative sample of participants more questions, and a small purposive sample of 5 a lot of in-depth questions.

The type of information needed drives the key decisions between representativeness and richness. Three central areas frame these considerations: complexity of questions, sensitivity of information needed, and availability of informants. As shown in Figure 6.1, as the complexity of the questions increases, the need for rich information increases as well. Similarly, if the questions are of a sensitive nature and people are unlikely to provide information unless they trust the data collector, then rich data collection procedures with few people are in order. Finally, with informants who are hard to locate or reluctant to answer evaluation questions, richer data collection strategies are indicated with fewer individuals.

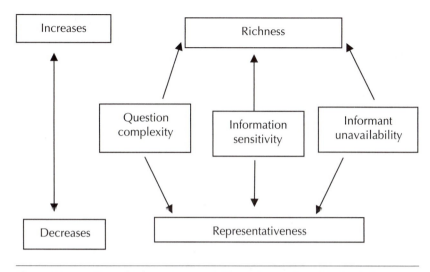

Figure 6.1   Type of Information Needs That Influence Sampling Strategies

Power is another consideration that influences sampling decisions. In essence, this means that evaluators want to collect enough information from individuals so that if a program component is having an effect they will be able to find it. Normally, the more people sampled, the more likely this is to happen. Another aspect of power (finding something occurring when it actually is) indicates that the greater the effect of the program, the fewer the individuals who need to be sampled. For quantitative studies that test statistical power, the level of significance used and the ability to predict either a positive or negative effect also influences power considerations. Kraemer and Thiemann (1987) and Lipsey (1990) are two sources for additional information about statistical power analysis.

Even when evaluation resources are plentiful, standards of good practice dictate optimizing data collection rather than maximizing it. Both the AEA's *Guiding Principles for Evaluators* (1995) and the Joint Committee on Standards' *Program Evaluation Standards* (1994) hold evaluators to the tenet of quality, cost-effective research practices. Collecting more information than is needed is a violation of this principle. Conducting a census when sampling will provide a more than adequate estimate of the total group opinion or characteristic is not defensible. On occasion, however, consulting everyone is appropriate. In the Volunteers Across America evaluation example, the evaluators did not need to consult all 250 programs to answer the evaluation questions. A mail survey of a representative sample would have met their needs for getting answers to the evaluation questions. The fact, however, that the program was new and that the program officers wanted to include everyone in the survey who was interested in providing them with feedback argued for inclusion of all 250 programs. This was a program dynamic that influenced the evaluation.

Sample Size

Answering the question, "How many people should I sample?" is similar to answering the question about how much an evaluation should cost. The answer is always the same: "It depends." It depends on a variety of factors among which the most important elements are the size of the entire group (population) under consideration, the questions that need answering, the resources available to the evaluation, and the amount of variation in the responses.

The generally accepted rule is that the more people you have in your group, the smaller the percentage of people you need to sample to find out what the whole group thinks. Although there are fairly involved procedures for calculating sample sizes (see, for example, Jaeger, 1984), for most evaluation purposes, adequate samples are easy to determine. Overall, people talk about 10% as a reasonable sample size; however, if you have a program with 30,000 participants or 30, the 10% rule is inappropriate. With 30,000, a sample of 3000 would be too many people, and if only 30 are in the group, a sample of 3 would be too few. The overriding issue is to sample sufficient numbers of people so that you capture sufficient information to answer the relevant evaluation questions.

The types of questions that need answering further influence the sample size question. As discussed earlier, rich data often take considerable amounts of time to collect. This could be because the data gatherer needs to build trust, ask probing questions, answer questions, and perform other time-consuming tasks. Thus, if multiple face-to-face interviews are needed, the evaluator will not be able to conduct as many as could be collected via a mail survey.

The resources available to the evaluation also will influence sample size. In those cases where evaluation resources are extremely limited, sample sizes will be on the modest side. In situations where the evaluation is more amply funded, sample sizes can be more robust. Another sample size consideration, related to evaluation resources, is who might be available to gather data. Sometimes it is extremely appropriate to engage program personnel as data gatherers. In other situations, particularly with multiple-language groups, availability of data gatherers might limit sample sizes.

Finally, the amount of variation in the actual group responses can influence sample sizes. In a situation where variation is great, including more people in the sample is usually a good idea. For example, a culturally diverse community would be expected to have more variation in its opinions about early childhood programs than one less culturally diverse. Normally, evaluators would make sure to gather sufficient data from the various groups to ensure their points of view are heard. Sometimes evaluators can anticipate variation; other times it is more problematic. In the case of the Volunteers Across America evaluation example, the survey data revealed unexpected differences by region among the 250 programs. The evaluators followed the mailed survey to all 250 programs with a telephone survey that sampled programs by region to see if they could identify the reasons for the differences.

Representativeness and Random Sampling Options

Why Random? The best chance anyone has of selecting a sample that is representative of a larger group is through randomizing the selection process. The overriding consideration is to avoid selection bias. Selection bias occurs when the findings represent the point of view of the particular group that was selected and not the larger group as a whole. For example, when school districts send home surveys with children for parents to fill out, they bias the sample to include parents who are literate and who have children who bring notes home. The school district does not really know what the other parents think.

Although randomizing selection procedures reduces the probability of selection bias, it does not guarantee it. If an evaluator randomly selects 10% of a group to survey, it could be that the group selected is not representative of the larger group. Usually, evaluators include relevant background questions on their surveys to establish how close the group surveyed is to the larger group. Another problem with randomized selection is that in some cases it can work against the process. Consider random selection of teachers to participate in an intensive series of interviews. Those teachers who consider the time needed for the interviews an imposition will probably find ways to avoid meeting or will provide as little information as they can. The evaluator will not gather their true opinions about the program, and thus the data will not even represent the individual, much less the group.

With these caveats, randomization of the selection process is still usually desirable. Four types of randomization procedures are described here briefly: simple random sampling, stratified random sampling, random cluster sampling, and systematic random sampling.

Simple Random Sampling. This method is the one that guarantees that each individual has an equal chance of being selected. There are more sophisticated ways to do this, but conceptually, this is the method in which all the names of group members are put in a hat and those names drawn indicate which individuals will participate. Unlike prize drawings, however, once someone's name is selected, it is replaced in the hat. Without this type of replacement, individuals, however slightly, have successively better chances of being selected. With Volunteers Across America, the database of the 250 programs was used in a statistical analysis program, and 75 programs were randomly selected.

Stratified Random Sampling. This method is used when there are subgroups of individuals within the groups that need to be included in the sample. The subgroups (strata) could be based on demographic factors such as county or gender. They also might be program-related factors, such as high-, medium-, and low-interest levels in reading. Whatever the strata, when selecting the sample, the idea is to first divide the individuals or programs by the strata and then randomly select the number needed from each of the division. With the Volunteers Across America example, the evaluators were interested in differences among five geographic regions and decided they needed a sample of 75 programs. They took the 250 programs, divided them by regions, and then randomly selected 15 programs per region. Alternatively, they could have sampled proportionally so that the number selected per region reflected the actual number of programs per region. They chose not to do this because they were interested in exploring the differences among regions, and had they sampled proportionally, as shown in Table 6.1, they would have had only 9 programs representing the northwest region.

Random Cluster Sampling. This method involves intact groups (e.g., classrooms, schools) that are randomly sampled as a whole. Often, when doing research across schools, clinics, or multisite programs, evaluators will randomly select entire units for participation in the data collection. Selecting four entire classrooms of 25 children within a school for study is usually less disruptive than randomly selecting 10 children from 10 classrooms. For example, with the Volunteers Across America program, evaluators could have randomly selected states and then included all the programs within that state; this would have been an example of random cluster sampling.

Systematic Random Sampling. This method uses a list of possible informants, starts randomly, and skips systematically to every *n*th person (depending on the number of people needed for the sample). It works well for large groups when there is a list of participants or programs. For Volunteers Across America, the list of 250 programs, organized alphabetically by program name, could have been used to randomly select a sample of 50 by starting randomly on the list and selecting every fifth program.

Purposive Sampling Options

Although selecting representative samples is good for some evaluation data collection needs, other data-gathering efforts require selecting individuals or

Table 6.1   Equal and Proportional Stratified Random Sampling for a Sample Size (N = 75)

Region	Number of Programs	Proportional Sample Size (N = 75)	Equal Sample Size (N = 75)
Northeast	60	18	15
South	50	15	15
Midwest	40	12	15
Northwest	30	9	15
Southwest	70	21	15

groups by preset criteria that would not be met by random selection methods. A host of purposive sampling options is available (see, for example, Gall, Gall, & Borg, 2003). These include selecting best-case examples, contrasting different variations within programs, and other possibilities. The evaluator needs to think through what is important to the evaluation and then select a purposive sampling strategy as appropriate. With Volunteers Across America, the program staff noticed differences by state that appeared linked to the number of programs within a state. Evaluators proposed to conduct 10 case studies (two per region) of states with high and low program density. High and low program density states were identified and grouped by the five geographic regions of interest. The evaluators reviewed this list of 20 states with the program staff to select the states and the specific programs within states that would be visited.

Combined Sampling Options

Mixing sampling strategies is not only possible but often indicated. Typically, lists of people are organized by other categories that lead to combining stratified random sampling with systematic random sampling. In the purposive sampling strategy described for Volunteers Across America, the evaluators started by stratifying the sampling by state, by region, and by program density. Only after that had been done did they sample purposively.

WAYS TO ADJUST SAMPLING PROBLEMS

Problems associated with sampling revert back to the issue of how well the selected informants (both randomly and purposively selected) represent the larger group from which they came. Random selection at any juncture limits evaluator-introduced sampling bias. Consequently, even within purposive sampling, randomizing selection procedure, where possible, increases the likelihood of representativeness.

One strategy to show that a sample is representative is to compare sample characteristics to the larger known population. This translates into identifying the relevant demographic and programmatic factors of the large group and the sample group. To the extent that these groups have similar proportions of men and women, of certain experience levels and within a specific age range, the evaluator can demonstrate comparability of the sample with the population.

In cases where low response rates threaten the representativeness of the sample, identifying a smaller random sample of nonrespondents and gathering information from them can go a long way toward establishing the responder sample's representativeness or lack thereof. If the smaller sample of nonresponders echoes the responses of the first sample, the evaluator can argue for limited sampling bias and, thus, the representativeness of the responder sample.

Instrument Selection or Development

The decision surrounding the selection of information-gathering strategies should be guided by the evaluation crosswalk questions and proposed information-gathering techniques and the type of information that needs to be collected (its complexity and possible sensitive nature). When instruments must be developed for evaluations, collaborative evaluators engage program staff in development. Further, collaborative evaluators review instruments with stakeholders as a way in which to validate appropriateness. This section reviews some of the more common data collection strategies used in evaluation and provides some examples of the more popular types. The section also discusses how to determine the validity and reliability of various evaluation instruments.

A word about terminology is warranted because, as usual, consistency in the field is lacking. For the purposes of this discussion, information-gathering strategies are the same as information-gathering techniques or sources. Both of these might be referred to as evaluation tools or instruments. Information and data are considered to be synonymous. Tests usually imply that there are correct and incorrect answers to questions, and opinion surveys usually assume there are neither right nor wrong answers in response to items (as opposed to questions). Attitude surveys usually intend to measure the strength of one or more opinions about things such as interest and satisfaction. Often, a collection of items is said to comprise a survey protocol. Questions in a survey, therefore, could also be called items in a protocol. The confusion among these terms is not intentional, it is just an artifact of usage.

USING THE EVALUATION CROSSWALK

Just as the evaluation crosswalk assisted in the sampling strategy selection, it can guide the selection of information-gathering choices. Together, the evaluation questions and the suggested information-gathering techniques will help the evaluator select appropriate measurement tools.

INSTRUMENT CHOICES

Instrument choices abound (see, for example, Gall, Gall, & Borg, 2003). For this section, however, only the most common instruments used in program evaluation have been selected for inclusion:

- Knowledge tests: Limited response, open-ended, performance assessment
- Opinion surveys: Written (on site, mail, e-mail, Web based), telephone, group interviews (including focus groups), individual interviews
- Attitude or interest surveys

Knowledge Tests. Knowledge tests assess differing degrees of content matter mastery. Bloom's taxonomy (Bloom, 1956) frames six cognitive domain areas—knowledge, comprehension, application, analysis, synthesis, and evaluation—which are today still acknowledged as circumscribing the territory of knowledge tests. In essence, knowledge tests come in three formats: limited response, open-ended response, and performance based. Tests to assess the first three levels of Bloom's taxonomy normally have correct and incorrect answers; assessments of higher order thinking are more subject to debate. Knowledge tests would be useful in an evaluation if one of the desired outcomes was to change knowledge levels. Knowledge-level tests may be scored relative to a comparison group (norm referenced) or relative to a set of standards (criterion referenced). Any test that reports a percentile score is norm referenced. Tests that speak to meeting licensure criteria or minimum competency are criterion referenced.

Limited Response. Limited response tests consist of those assessments in which the respondent chooses from available options. This category includes multiple choice, true-false, and matching. Limited response items are excellent for covering large amounts of content. They are challenging to construct but relatively easy to score.

Open-Ended. Open-ended tests ask respondents to generate the answers to questions. This category includes short answer and essay tests. This type of assessment lends itself well to assessing higher order thinking about content domain but is limited in how much content it can cover. A training program for health educators might want to assess the extent to which its trainees can develop and select curriculums for adolescents. Constructing open-ended tests is easier than limited response tests, but the scoring is more difficult.

Performance Assessment. Included in performance assessment are those groups of tests that require individuals to demonstrate their competence. The road test for a driver's license is a common performance assessment that many encounter. These assessments vary in the complexity of their construction and scoring, depending on the complexity of the behavior to be assessed. In an evaluation, if a program intended to improve the parenting practices of participants, a performance assessment to identify desired behavior changes might be appropriate.

Opinion Surveys. Opinion surveys ask respondents to share what they think about a variety of topics. They can share their opinions using limited response or open-ended formats. Normally opinions are neither right nor wrong and as such are not scored correct or incorrect. In program evaluation, opinion surveys are extremely prevalent (see Dillman, 1999, for a comprehensive discussion of mail and Internet surveys). Gathering feedback from participants about the different components of a program and how they are working would be an example of an opinion survey. Opinion survey information typically is gathered through one of four communication media: written surveys, telephone interviews, group interviews, and individual interviews.

Written surveys ask respondents to provide written responses to survey items. Respondents may do this on site while an evaluator or collaborating program staff member is present, through mailed-back responses, via e-mail, or (most recently) by way of Web-based surveys. Written surveys rely on the literacy of the respondent; therefore the literacy levels of respondents need to be considered very carefully.

Telephone surveys collect the desired information through phone questioning. Obviously, telephone surveys require that respondents have access to telephones. Although this was once a very popular way to gather opinion survey information, more recently the advent of answering machines and telemarketers has made this option more difficult, as people now screen calls more carefully.

A group interview occurs any time an evaluator asks a group for its opinion as a group. This is usually done through conversation with a facilitator leading the group and a second person taking notes. A focus group is a specialized version of a group interview that is intended to assess group opinion and probe for group consensus or disagreement.

Individual interviews are face to face and usually ask questions whose answers may be probed or further explored. Typically, when evaluators conduct individual interviews, they do so to explore the complexity of opinions and the reasons behind those opinions.

Attitude or Interest Surveys. Attitude or interest surveys ask respondents questions intended to assess the degree to which they hold a particular stance about something or their level of interest in it. They are very similar to opinion surveys, but unlike opinion surveys, which tend to report the number and type of responses, they seek to determine how strongly respondents feel about a particular topic. Most commonly, they will use a Likert-type scale (e.g., questions may be answered with "strongly agree," "agree," "disagree," "strongly disagree") or a semantic differential (e.g., answers may be given as ratings from "extremely interested" to "not interested") to assess the attribute of interest.

GUIDE TO INSTRUMENT SELECTION

Deciding which instrument to use depends on the evaluation, its need for information, and the available resources. Each of the data collection strategies described has advantages and limitations that should be consulted in making a selection. Table 6.2 lists data collection strategies with selection factors to consider. Discussion of these considerations with collaborating partners also helps the partners identify evaluation criteria.

In terms of format, limited response items take the least amount of response time, so relatively more items can be asked compared to the essay-style short answers of performance measures. At the same time, recognizing the response is not the same as generating the response. When the evaluator is unsure of possible options or desirous not to lead the respondent, using open-ended questions makes more sense. Performance assessments allow for the collection of information that demonstrates what people can do; the driving test to obtain a license is an example of a performance assessment. Portfolios are collections of information used to assess achievement. They can be used to showcase best performance, as in architecture or the performing arts. They also may be used to demonstrate progress over time.

With opinion surveys, wide geographic areas can be contacted via mail, telephone, e-mail, or the Web. Telephone survey questions generally need to be straightforward and relatively easy to answer as respondents do not have the questions before them to consult, and most people's auditory retention is limited. This is also true for questions that require serious thought before answering. Group surveys, including focus groups, can be useful for quick snapshots of what has occurred and as such are cost effective. Typically, the number of people to be sampled is fewer than with a written survey. During group and individual interviews, the evaluator also has the option of probing for details and of answering questions from the respondents. Individual

Table 6.2   Guide to Instrument Selection

Data Collection Strategy	Key Advantages	Limitations
Knowledge tests:	Assess content knowledge	
Limited response	Can cover large amount of content domain	Difficult to assess higher order cognitive skills
Open ended	Can assess higher order cognitive skills	Limited amount of content coverage
Performance assessment	Can assess actual behaviors	Resource intensive Limited amount of content coverage
Portfolios	Can showcase skills or show progress over time	Process needs management Limited amount of content coverage
Opinion surveys:	Assess opinions	
Written	Written record of responses	Need literate respondents
On site	Usually good response rates	Miss those not in attendance
Mail	Can contact people from different geographic areas	Poor response rates
E-mail	Ease of survey distribution	Respondents must have e-mail
Web based	Ease of survey distribution and data summary	Respondents must be able to use the Internet
Telephone	Can contact people from different geographic areas	Questions need to be easy to answer People reluctant to participate
Group	Cost effective Can assess degree of consensus	Limited number of participants in groups
Face to face	Can probe for more detail Respondents can ask questions	Resource intensive
Attitude and interest surveys	Assess degree of attitude or interest Easy to score	Little in-depth probing possible

interviews are particularly useful for gathering rich data or for interviews that require multiple visits. They are, however, resource intensive and thus usually indicate limited sample sizes.

VALIDITY AND RELIABILITY OF INSTRUMENTS

Validity is the extent to which a measurement is appropriate to its purpose. Reliability is the extent to which an assessment consistently elicits the same response or measurement. Reliability is necessary but not sufficient for validity; that is, a valid measurement must be reliable, but a measure may be reliable without being valid. A bathroom scale that gives one weight the first time you get on it and a different weight if you get off and then right back on it is unreliable (and probably broken). My favorite bathroom scale is very consistent (reliable), but unfortunately the weight it reports is 10 pounds less than my real weight. Alas, neither of my scales provides a valid measure of my weight.

Clearly, the validity and reliability of assessments used in evaluations is of great importance. It is a waste of evaluation resources to collect data that is not appropriate or that would change were the instrument to be administered a second time. Evaluators are responsible for ensuring that the instruments used are both valid and reliable.

Validity

The information to be collected determines the type of validity with which the evaluator must be concerned. Content-, construct-, and criterion-related validity comprise the three types of validity most commonly of interest in evaluations. Content validity asks the extent to which the assessment, often a test, covers the content of interest. This content domain could be an academic subject but also could be all the components of a program. Usually experts determine content validity. Construct validity asks the extent to which the assessment captures the construct of interest. Attitudes are constructs, as are satisfaction and school climate. Evaluators or other experts must consider the definition of the construct in determining construct validity. Criterion-related validity asks the extent to which the assessment is associated with an event in the future (predictive validity) or another instrument (concurrent validity). For example, the SAT test that many high school students take for college entrance is supposed to be predictive of first-year undergraduate grade point average. Paper and pencil measures of self-concept are expected to yield results similar to clinical assessments. Often, criterion-related validity is represented by a correlation coefficient usually designated as the letter r. The closer r is to one (either positive or negative one), the stronger the validity.

Reliability

Consistency of response, reliability, is usually measured with tests that have right and wrong answers and attitude measures, using one of three methods: test-retest, parallel forms, or internal consistency. *Test-retest* involves having the same group complete the assessment twice. In principle, enough time should pass between the two test administrations so that respondents cannot remember their responses. The amount of time between testings must also be sufficiently short that no learning has occurred. *Parallel forms* uses two equivalent assessments, and a group completes both assessments at one sitting. *Internal consistency* assumes parallel forms within a single assessment and estimates the consistency of responses.

With opinion surveys, reliability of instruments is usually established by having groups review the assessments to make sure that the direction, language, format, and content are clear.

PUBLISHED, UNPUBLISHED, OR DEVELOPED

The popular wisdom is that published instruments are usually better to use than unpublished instruments, which are usually better than evaluator-developed instruments. With this said, exceptions to this wisdom are common. Evaluation instruments are often program specific. Sometimes instruments are difficult to locate. Occasionally, published instruments exist, but their cost exceeds available evaluation resources. Evaluators must factor time and cost constraints into the decision to select published or unpublished instruments or develop an instrument specifically for the evaluation.

Published Instruments

Most published measurement instruments can be found in one of the 14 *Buros Mental Measurement Yearbooks,* which are indexed in *Tests in Print* (1999). These volumes can be found in most library reference sections. They may also be searched via the Internet at http://buros.unl.edu/buros/jsp/search.jsp.

Unpublished Instruments

Many unpublished instruments can be found in one of seven volumes of *Directory of Unpublished and Experimental Measures* (see, for example, Goldman & Mitchell, 1997). Evaluation reports of similar programs can provide excellent sources of unpublished measures. Finally, networking with programs that provide similar services often will lead to the sharing of useful evaluation instruments.

Table 6.3   Good Instrument Development Practices

A. Instrument choices
1. What types of information do you need to collect? (e.g., knowledge, opinions, attitudes, or interests)
2. What types of responses are needed? (e.g., limited responses, open-ended items, portfolios, performance measures)
3. How should the information be collected? (e.g., on site, mail, e-mail, Web based, telephone, group, face to face)
4. Who will be asked to provide the information?
5. What resources are available to collect the information?
6. Which types of responses are needed? (e.g., limited response, open ended)

B. Developing quality written questionnaires and interview protocols
1. Is the purpose of the instrument clear?
2. Are the directions clear?
3. Is the format inviting?
4. Does it allow for ease of response?
5. Is there enough space for responses?
6. Is the length respectful of respondents' time?
7. Is the information organized to ease data summary?
8. Are questions numbered?
9. Can it be machine scored?
10. Are limited response items used when appropriate?
11. Have you asked at the end, "Is there anything else you would like to share?"
12. Have you thanked participants for responding to the questionnaire?

Instruments Developed Specifically for the Evaluation

Many evaluations require the development of program-specific instruments. Consulting published or unpublished instruments first can provide ideas of what to assess, but on occasion, evaluators find that they must create entirely new instruments. When faced with this alternative, a number of key factors can improve the quality of the instrument. Table 6.3 lists a number of questions to answer that will help promote good instrument development practices.

FINDING VALIDITY AND RELIABILITY INFORMATION FOR PUBLISHED AND UNPUBLISHED INSTRUMENTS

If the evaluator selects published or unpublished instruments for the evaluation, the validity and reliability of those instruments must be established; this may occur either through previous validity and reliability testing or as part of the evaluation in which the instrument is currently being used. Published and unpublished instruments may or may not have previously established validity or reliability. When selecting an instrument, it is important to ascertain if validation studies have been done. Most publishers of assessments will let you know if this has been accomplished and should allow you access to the technical information, sometimes contained in a technical manual (which is different from the administration manual). With unpublished assessments, a literature search or contacting the author should provide the information needed about validity and reliability. If the instrument has not been validated for the evaluation purposes needed, the evaluator must pilot test it to establish its validity and reliability.

Ways to Pilot Test Instruments

Pilot testing takes the instrument identified or developed for the evaluation and tries it on a group of people similar to those in the sample. Because pilot testing can result in major instrument changes, it should not been done using sample subjects. Most pilot tests ask participants to complete the assessment and then comment on its appropriateness; this can be done in writing individually or through a group discussion. Comments are then used to modify the instrument. With published or unpublished instruments, revisions to the instruments usually cannot be done without the permission of the copyright holder. The pilot test responses also might be used to determine internal consistency reliability.

Collaborative Information Gathering

Instrument development, pilot testing, and validation build toward data collection. Garnering the cooperation of stakeholders to provide information is essential. A collaborative atmosphere will improve the amount and quality of information gathered.

PROMOTING PARTICIPATION

Data collection is another opportunity to engage stakeholders in the evaluation process. This participation is important from a technical standpoint, as it contributes to acceptable response rates. Participant engagement also can assist with improving the reliability of qualitative data.

INCREASING RESPONSE RATES

Good response rates are central to ensuring that the sample data collected are representative of the larger group of interest. Evaluators therefore must work hard to promote participation of stakeholders in data collection. Evaluators can encourage participation by (a) stressing the importance of the information requested, (b) reminding and encouraging people to participate, and (c) making the data collection process inviting.

Salience. The importance to the informant of the data to be gathered is the single best predictor of participation levels. In addition to communicating to the respondent the importance of the information, the following strategies can be employed that also will increase saliency: emphasizing the importance and uniqueness of the respondent, sending an endorsement letter from someone important to the respondent, sending an introductory letter to prepare the respondent for the data collection activity, and providing incentives.

Reminders. Reminders are another effective method of promoting participation in data collection. The current wisdom is that if you send out the first wave of surveys and 40% are returned without reminders, then half the initial response rate will come back with the first reminder (or 40% + 20% = 60%). Half that again will return with the second reminder, for a total of 70% (40% + 20% + 10% = 70%). Clearly, if the initial response rate is very low, reminders will not really help. For example, if 200 surveys are sent out and only 20 come back without reminders (a response rate of 10%), then with the first reminder an additional 5% will arrive, and an additional 2.5% will arrive with the second reminder. Continuing to send out reminders will not get the sample response rate up much above 17.5%.

Making the Data Collection Process Inviting. A third way to elicit stakeholder participation in data collection is by making the process inviting. Informants feel invited when they are treated respectfully, which includes respect for their time and effort. Refreshments make people feel invited, as does appreciation for their participation. Making written surveys graphically inviting is another strategy that will encourage people to participate in the data collection. Cluttered surveys that have confusing formats or directions "disinvite" people to respond.

Member Checking

Another way to promote collaboration with qualitative data collection is through a technique called "member checking." Qualitative data collection requires the person gathering the data to take notes or summarize transcribed field notes. Reliability can be a problem, as the evaluator is the filter for the data. The question becomes, "Had another conducted the interview, or the focus group, would the same data have been collected?" With member checking, the evaluator sends the transcripts or data summaries back to the informant to verify the contents. Having the informant check the contents and modify as needed increases the reliability of the information-gathering effort.

Example: The Rural Economic Development Program Focus Group

So far, this chapter has identified how data gathering in collaborative evaluation can be enhanced. It has also reviewed sampling and instrument development options. The following section presents an example—working from an evaluation crosswalk, followed by sample selection and instrument development—to provide the reader with a concrete application of the principles presented earlier.

This section uses the Rural Economic Development Program to examine the advantages of using focus groups to gather evaluation information, as well as highlighting some of the limitations accompanying this data collection strategy. This section also includes a discussion of how the program's evaluation context indicates focus groups as a data collection strategy, as well as detailing actual focus group protocols. The resultant data summaries from this focus group appear at the end of chapter 7, which focuses on collaborative data analysis. The very end of this section presents guidelines for using focus groups.

FOCUS GROUP STRENGTHS

For decades, market researchers have relied on focus groups to identify consumer preferences. For example, groups of shoppers were asked how they liked certain packaging of products or television watchers were asked to rate commercials. Since 1990, focus groups have increasingly been used in evaluation and social science research (see Krueger & Casey, 2000, for detailed information about focus groups).

Focus groups fall within the broader heading of group interview techniques. A few characteristics set focus groups apart from other group interview techniques. The evaluation or research purpose is fairly narrow or focused. Participants are selected based on a common experience or set of characteristics that is relevant to the evaluation or research purpose. Focus group facilitators are often interested in probing for group consensus or disagreement. Also, participants may initiate discussion or talk to others in the group rather than having the facilitator serving as the sole hub of the conversation wheel.

As with most group interview techniques, the use of focus groups is indicated when the following criteria or conditions are met: Questions are of moderate complexity; in-depth, detailed responses are important; group interaction is desirable; consensus or divergence about issues is of interest; categorical responses to questions are unknown, and the evaluator would like to identify a range of possible responses; information from other sources needs to be interpreted; respondents are unable to respond to written survey questions; and/or respondents would be uncomfortable responding to written survey questions.

Questions of Moderate Complexity

The nature of the evaluation question often indicates the most appropriate measurement technique, or at least rules out some as inappropriate. For example, if an evaluator wanted to answer the evaluation question, "How, if at all, did participants benefit from a year-long training program?" a focus group would be a reasonable measurement strategy. Further, if the program had multiple components and the evaluation required feedback on each of the components, the selection of a focus group would be even more appropriate as a measurement strategy.

Questions that can be answered with a yes or no response usually are not strong focus group questions. Similarly, other factors being equal, short answer questions with one- or two-word responses are best answered through written or telephone surveys. For a year-long training program, if all the evaluator needed to know was whether participants were interested in additional training, a focus group would not be necessary.

Table 6.4 presents the evaluation crosswalk from the Rural Economic Development Program example used previously. Notice that questions IA, IB, IIIB, and IIIC indicate that, in addition to other sources, focus groups will be used as a mechanism for gathering information. These four questions require some thought, and in the case of question IIIC, the evaluator must cover the multiple components of the foundation's support program.

Probing for Detail or Depth

Focus groups are recommended when evaluators expect to probe participants' responses for detail or ask respondents to expand their thinking. For example, for a year-long training program, an evaluator might begin with the desire to know *whether* participants believed they benefited from the program but would later want to pursue the details of *how* they benefited from the program. Similarly, the evaluator might need to explore how the contents of the training related back to participants' job needs.

In the example of the Rural Economic Development Program, question IA from the evaluation crosswalk, "To what extent have projects promoted rural

Table 6.4   Evaluation Crosswalk: Rural Economic Development Program

Data Sources

1 = Funding or refunding applications
2 = Site visit reports and foundation documents
3 = Grantees' internal evaluation documents
4 = Focus groups of grantee boards and staff
5 = Annual survey of grantees
6 = Case studies

Evaluation Questions	1	2	3	4	5	6
I. Enhanced economic development						
A. To what extent have projects promoted rural economic development?	X	X	X	X		
B. How have rural communities benefited from project activities?	X	X	X	X		
C. In what ways should the foundation modify its support of rural economic development?			X			
II. Strengthened infrastructure						
A. To what extent are projects using evaluation as a tool for keeping their activities effective?	X	X	X			
B. How have projects strengthened the capacity of rural communities?	X	X				
III. Collaborative work						
A. In what ways have grantees enhanced existing organizational and personal networks?		X			X	
B. How has enhanced networking promoted rural economic development?	X	X	X	X		
C. In what ways should the foundation modify its support of collaborative work?		X		X		

economic development?" is one that would require probing for detail. A potential response to the question might be, "It empowered community participants." Such a response needs to be probed so that the respondent's meaning is clear. A focus group facilitator might probe further by asking, "*How* did it empower community participants?"

Group Interaction Desirable

Often, focus group participation will stimulate recollections among participants or clarify their thoughts. What would not have been remembered for inclusion on a written survey will be remembered and shared in a focus group. What might never have been contemplated may be heard and then considered during a focus group.

Allowing focus group participants to comment and question each other can enrich the information gathered. For the Rural Economic Development Program example, the discussion about question IIIB might lead to participants discussing the merits of the cluster support group meetings sponsored by the foundation. Not all grantees participated in a cluster group, and each of the clusters had a different focus.

Group Consensus or Divergence of Interest

Focus groups provide an excellent vehicle for probing group consensus or divergence on a given topic. The facilitator might hear from several people with similar responses. If desired, the facilitator can then ask the group if they agree. In some instances, a facilitator might probe for the dissenting opinion, asking, "Is there anyone here who would disagree with that statement?"

Identifying the Range of Possible Responses

At times, categorical responses to questions are unknown, and the evaluator would like to identify the range of probable categories of responses. This type of focus group would be useful as a preliminary step to developing a written survey instrument. The evaluator could use a focus group or a set of focus groups to respond to potential survey questions as a method for both validating the question content and identifying possible responses. Most common responses can then be used to create a fixed response format for a written survey that is easier to summarize.

In the case of the Rural Economic Development Program, focus group responses to question IB, "How have rural communities benefited from project activities?" were summarized. Evaluators found that there were five categories of responses, and they included these on a written survey that was distributed to a sample of 100 cooperating agencies.

Interpreting Information From Other Sources

Sometimes focus groups greatly assist with the interpretation of data gathered from other sources. Survey results can pose challenging findings. Quantitative data summaries can suggest trends that are contextually not understood. Focus groups can refine, lend support, or dispel an evaluator's interpretation of findings.

Survey data collected from grantee board members as part of the Rural Economic Development Program evaluation revealed that grantees really liked the networking activities during the annual meeting but that after a year, fewer than 10% had any contact with members of the network. The evaluator was unclear as to why the grantee board members rated the networking highly but did not act on this interest. A focus group was scheduled with a representative sample of grantee board members to explore the reasons for the apparent contradiction. During the focus group, board members explained that much as they liked the networking opportunities, they just did not have the resources to organize follow-up contact. This information would not have been available had the focus group not been convened.

In another example with the Rural Economic Development Program, budget data led the evaluator to believe that no new communities had been added to one grantee's program, even though the majority of this member's grant from the foundation went to support a community outreach worker. Ostensibly, this fact would indicate that the program had not met its objective of expanding community outreach. The evaluator raised this finding during a focus group with the staff only to find that five new communities had been added. They did not appear in the budget statement because each of the five was sponsored by an existing partner program and under the partners' administrative umbrella.

Limited Literacy Skills Among Respondents

Evaluators are often faced with stakeholders who have much to contribute to the evaluation but who have limited literacy skills. Literacy rates in the United States are such that evaluators must be especially sensitive to their respondent audience's strongest communication mode. Evaluators (like many school districts that exclusively communicate with parents via written materials) should recognize this situation and consider focus groups instead of, or in combination with, written surveys.

Respondents' Discomfort With Written Formats

Some respondents, independent of basic literacy, are uncomfortable writing down their opinions. For those who are literate, often their ability to speak excels their ability to write; they would rather share their opinions orally, in a more fluid manner. Another portion of the population is suspicious of committing opinion to paper. They may initially view evaluators with suspicion and withhold information that is asked for in a survey. Often they feel more comfortable with a face-to-face interaction and will readily share the information during a focus group setting. Others (e.g., high school dropouts, academically at-risk students) equate writing with schooling and refuse to revisit unpleasant memories. In these cases, the evaluator should opt for focus groups as the preferred data collection method.

FOCUS GROUP LIMITATIONS

Focus groups are limited in a number of ways. Participants are influenced by each other. It is impossible to know what they might have said independently. Occasionally, individuals can divert focus groups, monopolize group time, or sway opinion. The quality of a focus group is often determined by the quality of the facilitator. Also, representativeness of focus group findings must be verified.

Participants Are Influenced by Each Other

The focus group can influence how people think about their experience in a program. It is impossible to know what participants might have said independently. If this is an important consideration, then you might, assuming a high literacy level, ask them to complete a short written survey just prior to the meeting of the focus group.

Individuals Can Divert Focus Groups

People with strong personalities and those who like to talk monopolize the focus group time. These people also may sway opinion by the force of their belief or through the reluctance of others to disagree. This problem can accelerate in situations where participants are of unequal stature (e.g., a principal is participating in a focus group with teachers or an executive director is participating in a focus group with staff).

Facilitator Quality

The quality of a focus group is often determined by the quality of the facilitator. The facilitator is the key to gathering good focus group results. Some focus groups are easier than others (e.g., the questions are easily fielded by the participants, the topic is not politically charged, the group dynamics are good). Other focus groups can prove difficult. A strong facilitator is essential for difficult focus groups.

Verifying Findings

Due to less than ideal sampling techniques and the real difficulty of guaranteeing a high rate of participation by those invited to focus groups, the degree to which focus group information is representative of the larger population is extremely important and often questionable. Evaluators and researchers must find some way to verify findings; this activity often is referred to as triangulation. Multiple focus groups can help, as can other data sources that corroborate focus group findings. If evaluators conduct three focus groups and find three different sets of emerging themes, this is not triangulation of findings. To triangulate the findings and verify the fidelity of the information (the extent to which the information collected actually represents reality), each of the three sets of themes must be investigated. This activity is similar to journalistic verification. If a reporter consults three sources and each provides different information, the information from each of the sources in turn must be confirmed. Had all sources agreed, then the reporter could have assumed the information was accurate.

RURAL ECONOMIC DEVELOPMENT
FOCUS GROUP SAMPLE SELECTION

As part of a 3-day annual gathering for Rural Economic Development Program grantees, focus groups were conducted with grantees by two members of the evaluation team. The gathering was selected for the focus groups site because most grantees attended, and therefore travel costs would be minimized, creating a cost-effective data gathering opportunity. Gathering organizers also were amenable to scheduling the focus groups so that conflict with other planned activities would be minimized.

The purpose of the focus groups was to gather evaluation information about how the funding program was working, thereby providing information about the foundation's procedures and support services and how they might be improved. Further, these focus groups were intended to allow an opportunity for evaluators to probe grantees' beliefs about what the programs were accomplishing regarding the promotion of rural economic development. These areas were represented in the evaluation crosswalk by questions IA and IIIC. Other focus groups would be held during the year to address the other evaluation questions that called for focus group information. Two cohorts of grantees would be present (Cohort 1, those organizations in their second year of the 3-year funding program, and Cohort 2, those organizations completing their first year of funding). Additionally, staff from the organizations and board members normally attended the gathering.

Cohort 1 and Cohort 2 grantee staff members were divided into two groups by cohort; grantee board members were divided similarly. The resulting four focus groups lasted from 30 to 60 minutes each. Of the two focus groups held for Cohort 1 grantee staff members, 9 of 12 staff member groups were represented in one group (2 attended from the other group) and 12 of 14 in the other. Of the two focus groups held for Cohort 1 grantee board members, 10 of 13 board member groups were represented in one group and 9 of 12 in the other.

Cohort 2 grantees were divided into two groups alphabetically by their organization's name, and two focus groups also were held for Cohort 2 grantee staff members. The focus groups lasted from 15 to 20 minutes each. Twelve of 13 groups were represented in one group, and 11 of 12 groups were represented in the other.

RURAL ECONOMIC DEVELOPMENT
PROGRAM FOCUS GROUP PROTOCOL

A focus group protocol, also called a focus group guide, was drafted following the key questions identified in the evaluation crosswalk. Because multiple focus groups would be conducted, uniform procedures were important to ensure that participants were provided with consistent opportunities to provide information. Of the two evaluation team members, one would serve as facilitator and the other as recorder. Had there been different focus group facilitators across groups, specification of uniform procedures would have been even more important.

The purpose of the focus group and the rules of procedure, as well as the questions, were contained in the protocol. Once drafted, the foundation staff reviewed the focus group protocol to make sure that the questions being asked were appropriate to the program and the evaluation purpose. Additionally, members of the evaluation team reviewed the protocol for clarity. Questions were then pilot tested with two grantees who would not be able to attend the gathering.

All of these activities aimed toward ensuring that validity and reliability of the protocol was acceptable. In this case, the validity issue focused primarily on ensuring that the content of the focus group questions was consistent with the purpose of the evaluation, that no important questions were omitted, and that no unnecessary questions were included. Reliability requires that focus group participants understand the questions sufficiently so that they would respond similarly if asked to respond to the same question again, assuming no change in experience. To accomplish this, evaluators made sure that the language used was appropriate and the questions asked were unambiguous. Finally, evaluators identified a group similar to the actual focus groups and had the members answer and review the questions, which further established the instrument's validity and reliability.

Once the instrument was developed, the evaluators shared copies of the instrument with potential focus group participants. This practice allows participants to view the questions ahead of time and reflect on their answers. It also permits those invited to gage the intent of the information-gathering activity.

Figure 6.2 presents the focus group protocol for the Rural Economic Development Program. Minor changes were made to the instrument for the

Rural Economic Development Program
FOCUS GROUP PROTOCOL: Cohort 2

Your Role (circle one): Staff   Board   Your Group (circle one):   A   B

Hello, my name is _____, and I would like to thank you for coming to this focus group. The purpose of this focus group is to find out what you think about the foundation's support procedure and activities, as well as your program accomplishments this year. We sent a copy of the focus group questions to your organization last month. Another copy of the questions should be in front of you now.

I will be facilitating the discussion. My colleague, _____, will serve as recorder. We guarantee to you that your responses will be treated as confidential. That means that the summary of this focus group will not reveal your identity. We would like to record the proceeding so that we do not miss any information. If no one objects, I will turn the recorder on now. [Wait for objections, and proceed accordingly.]

Just so that everyone is clear about how this focus group works, let me explain what will happen. I expect this session to last no more than 30 minutes. Let's review the ground rules. First, I will serve as the facilitator, asking questions and recognizing people as they offer to speak. Second, only one person may speak at a time. Finally, as long as you don't disrupt the discussion, you may move around the room and help yourself to refreshments.

Are there any questions? [Wait for questions, and proceed accordingly.]

1a. The foundation recognizes that you are all very busy people. What, if anything, did you find useful about completing the application?

1b. How might the application process be improved?

2a. What, if anything, did you find useful about foundation support for the grant?

2b. How might foundation support be improved?

3. What do you expect this year's economic community development grant to accomplish for your organization?

4. At this time, is there anything else you would like to add?

Thank you for your time.

Figure 6.2   Focus Group Protocol

rates from those selected, as more people connected with the program understand the purpose of the data gathering. After reviewing instrument options, ways to engage stakeholders in instrument development were shown to include reviewing draft instruments, pilot testing of instruments, sharing of instruments with respondents before data are actually gathered, and member checking to make sure data collected via the researcher actually reflect what the respondent wanted to say. Finally, the chapter presented an example of data collection, from an evaluation crosswalk to data gathering for a focus group needed for the Rural Economic Development Program evaluation.

two different cohort groups. To facilitate note taking, these pro†
expanded, with more space allowed between questions.

Guidelines for Using Focus Groups

1. Prepare questions prior to the meeting of the focus group, an
   for clarity.

2. Make sure that the focus group questions are consistent wit
   plan.

3. Keep focus groups to no more than 10 to 12 people.

4. Be considerate of participants' time, mental fatigue level, and

5. Form focus groups of people with common background
   levels, age, income, role in organization).

6. Generally limit the time of a focus group to an hour or l
   tiring. Always give participants a best estimate of how long
   expected to last.

7. Consider providing focus group members with a copy c
   questions.

8. A facilitator and a recorder should assist with the focus gr

9. At the beginning of a focus group, all participants should
   purpose of the focus group reviewed, and the ground rule
   the focus group will operate.

10. Focus group participants should be informed about th
    their responses.

11. Evaluators should obtain participant permission before

12. At the end of a focus group meeting, always allow people
    believe to be germane, and thank them for their time.

13. Pilot testing mock focus groups can provide practice o
    perienced facilitators and improve the quality of the fo

Summary of Collaborative Data Gathering

This chapter presented the planning stage of collabora
explaining how collaborative evaluators work to engage
collection efforts. It reviewed sampling strategies availab
emphasized that collaborative evaluation often makes
frames easier, as program staff can help to identify various i
groups. Collaborative evaluation also contributes to fa

7

Collaborative Data Analysis

ata analysis is summarizing information. Once evaluation data have
been collected, they are organized in ways that will answer evaluation
questions, which are the research equivalent of hypotheses. The questions to be
answered and the type of data collected will determine how the information is
summarized. Just as data collection can be done collaboratively, data analysis
can be done in ways that engage stakeholders in the process.

This chapter reviews common quantitative and qualitative data analysis
approaches in the context of the evaluation questions that they answer. It
also discusses how computer software programs can greatly aid in analysis.
Collaborative data analysis strategies are suggested, and examples using both
types of techniques demonstrate how to apply data analysis strategies in
evaluation situations.

Matching Evaluation Questions to Analysis Strategies

The types of questions to be answered and the data collected to answer those
questions determine what types of analyses are possible. Test scores, and other
things that can be counted, result in quantitative summaries. Focus group discussions and interview notes yield qualitative summaries. Using multiple data
sources and their accompanying analyses to depict a program yields a much
more robust answer to evaluation questions than does a single data source
solution.

QUANTITATIVE QUESTIONS AND ANALYSIS

Quantitative questions involve things that you can count. The question,
"How many people participated in the program?" is quantitative. To answer it,

an evaluator must set up a system to collect information on the number of individuals who participated. This could be done using enrollment sheets, attendance lists, staff notes, or any other system that would yield the desired information. At the end of some specified time frame, the information on participation is gathered and the data analyzed to produce one number that represents the total number of individuals participating in the program.

These types of analyses are so common that people rarely consider that they are conducting quantitative analyses when they report service statistics. Collecting other frequency data and calculating means, modes, and medians are similarly viewed. Be warned: frequencies (f), means (M), modes (Mo), and medians (Mdn) are statistics. Many people who claim no knowledge of statistics use these (both the words and the numbers the words denote), as they are not aware that they are statistics. They are, however, part of quantitative analyses in evaluation.

The mystique of statistics—that they are "too technical" for ordinary people to understand—persists, with the assistance of many who were academically abused in elementary or middle school and led to believe that they cannot do math. Although statistics may not be the easiest subject on the planet, evaluators do not need a degree in mathematics to understand common statistical procedures and how to use them in evaluations. In fact, computer software is such that math-challenged people can now complete analyses with relative ease.

Descriptive statistics describe group characteristics. Inferential statistics make statements about groups based on information from samples. Sample statistics are tested to see whether observations are due to systematic differences or random occurrences. It is important to note that these systematic significant differences can be very small. Thus evaluators must interpret statistical significance to determine how substantial the differences may or may not be. Where appropriate, calculations of effect size are slowly replacing significance levels as the statistic of interest. Effect size reports how much difference there is between groups on pre- and posttests in terms of a proportion of the range of possible change, usually a standard deviation (the average distance from the mean of all the scores or measurements). With normal distributions, the range of scores is about six standard deviations long. An effect size of $+1.0$ means that the treatment group out performed the control group by one standard deviation. This would be a sizable effect for the treatment. It would be the equivalent of one group scoring 500 (50th percentile, average) on the SAT and the other group scoring 600 (84th percentile, well above average).

A few words of caution: Do not be led astray by people who argue, "You can make numbers say anything you like." Numbers are no different than words. Unless evaluators misrepresent reality by altering figures, which would be the equivalent of putting words into people's mouths, numbers can only be analyzed so far. Evaluators may clean data, scrub variables, massage and even sometimes torture numerical data, but the truth is that numbers are no more manipulable than words.

Table 7.1 shows common quantitative evaluation questions and the statistics that accompany them. For each of these statistical tests, the researcher sets the alpha (usually at .05) and finds the value of the statistic (e.g., r, t, or F). With statistical computer programs (e.g., the Statistical Package for the Social Sciences [SPSS] and Statistical Analysis System [SAS]) the statistic will be shown with a probability. If the probability shown on the printout is equal to or less than the alpha level, the statistic is said to be "significant." If no probability is given, the researcher takes the calculated statistic and goes to a table of critical values for the selected statistic, which can be found in some educational research texts. Then the researcher finds the critical value of the statistic for the appropriate degrees of freedom. If the calculated statistic is equal to or larger than the critical value statistic, then the statistic is said to be significant.

QUALITATIVE QUESTIONS AND ANALYSIS

Qualitative questions yield information in words that need to be summarized. Quantitative questions are fairly uniform across disciplines, but qualitative questions are not. Asking about the differences between two groups on a knowledge test is the same in sociology as it is in medicine. Qualitative questions, however, are influenced by the qualitative approach being used and carry with them assumptions that are discipline specific.

Table 7.2 lists the more common qualitative approaches by discipline, followed by a typical question that might be asked. Notice that with ethnography, issues of culture are central, just as with history, questions about the past apply. Much more confusion exists about qualitative than about quantitative approaches, in part because training in qualitative methods has been more limited than for quantitative methods. Another source of confusion stems from the fact that the different approaches share many of the same data collection methods. Interviews, focus groups, and observation are common across all qualitative approaches. Occasionally, people group these information-gathering techniques under one indistinguishable qualitative umbrella and lose important discipline distinctions.

Qualitative data may be analyzed in a host of ways (see, for example, Miles & Huberman, 1994). Among data analysis possibilities, content analysis is by far the most commonly employed strategy. With content analysis, open-ended survey responses, field notes, interviews, and so on are reviewed so that information may be organized in such a way that it will answer the evaluation questions. Usually, the evaluator will collect the data and then conduct separate analyses for each data collection strategy involved. With each data collection

Table 7.1   Common Quantitative Approaches: Linking Evaluation Questions to Analysis Choices

Evaluation Questions	Number of Groups	Number of Measures	Statistic	Degrees of Freedom
Correlation: A systematic, linear relationship between two variables (e.g., as one goes up, the other goes up) Q: Is there a relationship between SAT scores and first-year college GPAs?	1	2 (e.g., SAT and GPA)	Correlation coefficient (r)	$n - 2$
Paired t test or t test for nonindependent samples: Difference between two means Q: Do students do better on the posttest than on the pretest?	1	Pretest Posttest	Paired t test (t)	$n - 1$
t-test for independent samples: Difference between the means of two groups Q: Does the treatment group do better than the comparison group on the outcome measure?	2	Outcome measure	t test for independent samples (t)	$n_1 + n_2 - 2$
ANOVA: Difference among means where there are three or more groups Q: Does group 1 do better than group 2 or group 3 on the outcome measure?	3 or more	Outcome measure	ANOVA (F)	k (groups) $- 1$, $n - k - 1$
ANCOVA: Difference among means where there are three or more groups, controlling for a confounding variable. Q: Does group 1 do better than group 2 or group 3 on the outcome measure, controlling for previous achievement?	3 or more	Outcome measure, covariate measure	ANCOVA (F)	k (groups) $- 1$, $n - k - 1$

Note: ANCOVA = analysis of covariance; ANOVA = analysis of variance; F = statistic reported with ANCOVA and ANOVA; GPA = grade point average; k = number of groups or factors; n = number of people in the sample, n_1 = number of people in group 1; n_2 = number of people in group 2; r = correlation coefficient; t = statistic calculated for paired or independent t tests.

Table 7.2   Common Qualitative Data Analysis Approaches

Approach	Discipline	Possible Questions	Possible Data Methods
Phenomenology	Philosophy	What is the nature of the program?	Observations Interviews Symbolic interactions
Ethnography	Anthropology	How does the program's culture influence success?	Participant observations Knowledgeable informants Oral traditions Interviews Field notes
Historiography	History	How do current events fit with previous ones?	Primary archival documents Oral history Interviews Narratives
Naturalistic inquiry	Education	What occurs daily in the program?	Observations Interviews Field notes
Case study methods	Clinical medicine	What are the issues relevant to this program?	Observations Interviews Field notes Vignettes
Grounded theory	Sociology	What social systems are operating within this program?	Observations Interviews Sociograms Theory formulation
Investigative reporting	Journalism	What is the real story behind why this program is so successful?	Interviews Telephone inquiries Protected sources Background research

strategy, then, the evaluator groups responses together for each item. Within items, similar responses are grouped together, and each of these groups is assigned a name that captures the similarity. Once this is accomplished for each data source, analyses may occur across sources.

Using the Computer to Assist With Analysis

Computers can assist with both quantitative and qualitative data analysis. Spreadsheet programs such as *Microsoft Excel* can provide analysis assistance with limited data sets; this is true for both quantitative and qualitative data.

As the amount and type of data increase in complexity, more specialized programs are advisable. *Access,* included with *Microsoft Office,* is a database program that keeps track of different sorts of information (data fields) by individual or program. It is especially useful when the information needs to be sorted in a variety of ways and levels. *Excel* and *Access* work very well at keeping up with information and reporting service statistics (e.g., number of people served, zip codes of participants). Specialized statistical and qualitative analysis computer programs, however, can be of tremendous assistance for summarizing information beyond the monitoring basics.

QUANTITATIVE COMPUTER ANALYSIS SOFTWARE

In evaluation, SPSS and SAS are the two most commonly used statistical analysis software programs. Differences between the two are minimal, and the choice is usually made based on familiarity or access. Over the years, these programs, like most software, have become progressively easier to use; the cost, as well, has come down. Information about the two can be found at http://www.spss.com and http://www.sas.com on the Internet. The decision to use a statistical analysis program should be determined by the evaluation's ongoing data analysis needs. Securing the assistance of a statistical analysis consultant also is a possibility for beginning evaluators.

To use quantitative software to analyze data, the information must be in an electronic format. Normally, data are entered into columns for each person assessed. This is an easy task to do if the data are already in *Excel,* or evaluators can set up tables in *Microsoft Word.* Data also may be directly entered in the statistical software program, but editing capabilities are usually better in *Excel* or *Word.*

QUALITATIVE COMPUTER ANALYSIS SOFTWARE

Qualitative data collection strategies generate huge amounts of information. Organizing that information so that it is available for multiple analyses is extremely important. Qualitative data analysis software can now assist greatly with the analysis process, although this was not true 10 years ago. Non-Numerical, Unstructured Data Indexing, Searching, and Theorizing (*NUD.IST*) and *Atlas-ti* are two qualitative data analysis programs that were specifically developed for analyzing qualitative data. These are specialized database management programs that are similar to *Access* or a spreadsheet program like *Excel* but have many specialized properties that facilitate qualitative data analysis. Information about *NUD.IST* and *Atlas-ti* is available at http://www.sagepub.com on the Internet.

Using qualitative software requires that the data be in an electronic format. Both *NUD.IST* and *Atlas.ti* will accept *Microsoft Word* text files.

One of the advantages of using a qualitative analysis program over *Excel* is that it includes specialized tasks that make qualitative data analysis simpler. For example, if you have a six-question, open-ended survey, you can ask the program to gather all responses from question 1 and put them together automatically in their own file. In *Excel,* the only way to do this is to cut and paste the responses.

Once data are imported into the programs, the evaluator can go through and code the information. Coding just means taking a response and deciding if it is consistent with other responses and grouping similar responses together. Usually the evaluator will name the similarity among the responses to keep the analysis organized. Coding can be done using preexisting codes, emerging codes, or a combination of both. The software program will group similar responses and keep track of which data files provided those responses.

In the example shown in Figure 7.1, the evaluator completed 25 interviews with participants to find out how the two project outcomes were being met. Responses were coded by placing comments related to Objective 1 in the Objective 1 grouping and comments related to Objective 2 into the Objective 2 file. The evaluator placed unintended outcomes into a grouping called "other outcomes." Within Objective 1, two themes emerged, and comments were divided according to these two themes. Objective 2 saw three themes emerge. No further coding was done with the other outcomes. The evaluator also was interested in knowing which people had comments that represented both Theme C and Theme D. Those were combined into a composite theme, Composite 1. Normally, an evaluator will print out the contents of each category grouping (called a node in *NUD.IST*) and then use that summary to write up the summary report for those interviews.

Using Stakeholders to Assist With Analysis

Stakeholders can provide enormous help in analyzing data. This assists the evaluator in reducing external resources needed to summarize the evaluation information and allows stakeholders to see what happens to the information they provide.

As with the other aspects of collaborative evaluation, discussions about stakeholder involvement begin in the planning stages of the evaluation and continue through implementation. In some cases, certain program staff members may have the necessary capability to analyze most of the information collected. In other cases, stakeholders can be easily trained to assist with data analysis. Yet again in other situations, the collaborative evaluator will be the one to summarize the information. Once again, the key to successful collaborative evaluation is communication with the client about the desirability and availability of stakeholder involvement in data analysis.

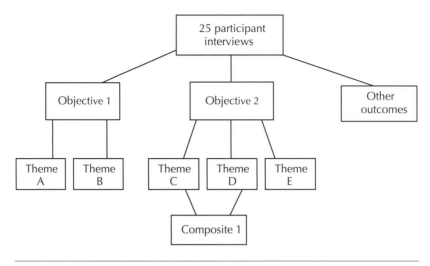

Figure 7.1   Qualitative Data Analysis Coding Example

Often quantitative data are very elementary in nature, and most stakeholders have the expertise to help. Summarizing frequencies of client satisfaction ratings does not require graduate school training. Similarly, many staff can calculate averages for knowledge test results on paper and pencil measures. Stakeholders also can conduct more complicated analyses with training and assistance. One program manager used the evaluation as an opportunity to acquire SPSS for the organization and had the evaluators train her in its operation, as she assumed responsibility for summarizing attitudinal change data about their clients.

Collaborative opportunities also abound for collaborative qualitative data analysis. Program staff and other stakeholders bring considerable understanding and insight about program dynamics. They can greatly assist evaluators in developing coding schema prior to content analysis. Further, they can be included in training to code qualitative responses. Stakeholders also can specify how much detail they desire in the depth of analysis, which guides the evaluator in deciding the level of data specificity desired (e.g., whether or not to include individual comments with summaries of qualitative data sources).

One example of collaborative data analysis occurred with students and teachers at a school that had just completed a needs assessment for future planning. Rather than have the evaluators whisk the surveys off to analyze them, teachers at the school agreed to extend the homeroom period to work with the students to summarize the information. Before the students saw the surveys, evaluators met with participating teachers and discussed what needed to be done. Teachers and evaluators both offered suggestions about how the process might work and the best way to do it. This planning group also decided that two different groups would independently summarize each section of the survey, thereby allowing a means to verify findings. Evaluators summarized what had been agreed to during the meeting and sent teachers a copy of that summary. Evaluators also prepared the materials needed for the data summaries and distributed them to the teachers. Different sections of the survey were distributed to different homeroom groups, each was summarized, and then each group prepared a presentation to the rest of the school. Resultant ownership of the data was extremely powerful, and the entire school participated in a planning event based on the needs assessment data summaries.

An observation is offered here for skeptical readers who believe that having stakeholders involved in analysis is probably more fraught with problems than not. Collaborative evaluation is conducted with stakeholders who are interested in finding out the answers to the evaluation questions that they have identified as important. In fact, almost everyone who works in social programs genuinely tries to do the right thing. No one wants to waste time working for programs that are ineffective. If stakeholders view the evaluation as useful to them, their participation in data analysis will be honest and forthright. Those who believe that data analysis is beyond the objectivity or capacity of stakeholders should rethink their position. People who are interested in evaluation outcomes will participate as best they can to the extent they are offered the opportunity. This is as true for evaluation assistants as it is for stakeholders. They also should be expected to communicate about their ability (or lack thereof) to complete analysis tasks.

Quantitative and Qualitative Analysis Examples

In the sections that follow, the Rural Economic Development Program evaluation is used to provide examples of both quantitative and qualitative analysis within an evaluation context. These examples are included to provide the reader with applications of the strategies included in the first part of this chapter.

QUANTITATIVE EXAMPLE: RURAL ECONOMIC DEVELOPMENT PROGRAM

Recall that, as shown in the abbreviated crosswalk in Table 7.3, the Rural Economic Development Program evaluation called for an annual survey of grantees to collect information about enhanced collaboration. At the end of the first program year, the first ten grantees completed the survey. At the end of the second year, these same grantees provided similar information, and the second cohort of ten provided information about their first year of the grant.

Table 7.3   Rural Economic Development Program Evaluation
Crosswalk Questions for Annual Collaboration Survey

Evaluation Questions	1	2	3	4	5	6
III. Collaborative work						
A. In what ways have projects enhanced existing organizational and personal networks?		X			X	X

Note: Source of data for question 5 was the annual survey of grantees.

A section of the survey asked grantees to list collaborating organizations and the types of collaboration occurring. Each organization could have multiple types of collaborative relationships with each of the grantees. Plans to collect additional information included site visit reports and case studies. To determine whether collaboration increased from Year 1 to Year 2, based on the survey data, the evaluator first organized the information from the grantees in Cohort 1 as shown in Table 7.4.

As shown in the compiled data, totals for all three types of collaboration have increased. Each of the ten grantees increased in at least one category (three increased in one category, three increased in two, and four increased in all three categories). Four of 30 possible categories showed decreases, five remained the same, and the rest all improved.

Another way to look at the data would be to summarize the information by type of referral by year. Table 7.5 provides means and standard deviations (*SD*s) for the same data. Just looking at the means might lead someone to say that each category had increased systematically. A *t* test for paired samples would be a way to check and see if the differences observed are more than what might be expected due to randomly expected variation. (Go back to Table 7.1 to determine why the paired *t* test is most appropriate and not another statistical test.) SPSS reveals that only two of the three sets of mean differences between Year 1 and Year 2 are significantly different. With an alpha level probability set at less than or equal to .05, the difference in collaboration from Year 1 to Year 2, although increased by five in terms of "work together toward common goal," is not significant.

Another way to analyze the data would be to calculate an effect size for each of the changes. Table 7.6 shows the means and standard deviations for the pairs with the combined standard deviation for each of the collaboration types. Effect size was calculated as the difference in the means divided by the combined standard deviation. It corroborates the earlier

Table 7.4   Number of Collaborating Organizations by Type of Collaboration

Cohort 1	Make Referrals To		Receive Referrals From		Work Together Toward Common Goal	
	Year 1	Year 2	Year 1	Year 2	Year 1	Year 2
Grantee 1	7	12	4	6	3	5
Grantee 2	12	11	18	22	5	5
Grantee 3	2	6	10	12	2	3
Grantee 4	0	0	12	14	7	6
Grantee 5	16	14	5	4	1	2
Grantee 6	4	7	8	11	9	9
Grantee 7	10	10	3	4	3	3
Grantee 8	7	9	6	6	0	2
Grantee 9	9	12	0	0	2	2
Grantee 10	13	15	11	16	10	10
Totals	80	96	77	98	42	47

Table 7.5   Means, Standard Deviations, and t Statistics by Type of Collaboration for Cohort 1

Cohort 1 (n = 10 grantees)	End Year 1 Mean (SD)	End Year 2 Mean (SD)	t (Probability)
Make referrals to	8 (5.03)	9.6 (4.40)	5.03 (.001)
Receive referrals from	7.7 (5.23)	9.8 (6.83)	2.91 (.017)
Work together toward common goal	4.2 (3.43)	4.7 (2.91)	1.63 (.138)

Table 7.6   Effect Size Calculation by Type of Collaboration for Cohort 1

Cohort 1 (n = 10 grantees)	End Year 1 Mean (SD)	End Year 2 Mean (SD)	Combined SD	Effect Size
Make referrals to	8 (5.03)	9.6 (4.40)	4.67	.34
Receive referrals from	7.7 (5.23)	9.8 (6.83)	6.02	.35
Work together toward common goal	4.2 (3.43)	4.7 (2.91)	3.10	.16

t-test finding that revealed no significant differences with the third type of collaboration. Further, it shows that the difference in making referrals to other organizations and receiving them from other organizations has the same level of impact.

QUALITATIVE EXAMPLE OF RURAL ECONOMIC DEVELOPMENT PROGRAM

Recall that, as shown in the highlighted sections of Table 7.7, the Rural Economic Development Program evaluation convened focus groups of grantees to collect information about enhanced economic development and collaborative work.

Six questions guided the development and selection of focus group questions:

1a. The foundation recognizes that you are all very busy people. What, if anything, did you find useful about completing the application?

1b. How might the application process be improved?

2a. What, if anything, did you find useful about foundation support for the grant?

2b. How might foundation support be improved?

3. What do you expect this year's economic community development grant to accomplish for your organization?

4. At this time, is there anything else you would like to add?

Table 7.7   Rural Economic Development Program Evaluation Crosswalk Questions for Focus Group

Evaluation Questions	1	2	3	4	5	6
I. Enhanced economic development						
A. To what extent have projects promoted rural economic development?	X	X	X	X		X
B. How have rural communities benefited from project activities?	X	X	X	X		X
C. In what ways should the foundation modify its support of rural economic development?		X			X	
III. Collaborative work						
A. In what ways have projects enhanced existing organizational and personal networks?		X			X	X
B. How has enhanced networking promoted rural economic development?	X	X	X	X		
C. In what ways should the foundation modify its support of collaborative work?		X		X	X	

Note: Data for answers to question 4 came from focus groups of grantee boards and staff.

As soon as possible after the focus group meeting ends, both facilitator and recorder should complete their field note records. Field notes are comments about the focus group that are important to the summary of the information. They may include a description of the group or notes about particularly harmonious interactions and areas of group consensus or divergence.

Much of the data summary time will be spent in the transcription of comments. With fairly rapid typing, 20 minutes of focus group discussion can take 2 hours to transcribe. Table 7.8 displays the comments from the two staff focus groups for the first question about the application process for the Rural Economic Development Program. Notice that individuals have been given a letter identification code so that the researcher may track comments across individuals and, in this case, their roles. For example, 1Sa is the first (1) staff person (S) from the first staff focus group (a) to comment during the focus group. This is extremely important, as comments often contain multiple themes that will later be extracted. To judge whether focus group comments represent the entire group of participants or just a few, the evaluator must track comments by person. In this manner, the summary can reflect how many organizations or people expressed similar sentiments. Further, in this case, the evaluator anticipated the need to separate staff (S) comments from those of board (B) members due to acknowledged differences in their participation in the application process.

Rural Economic Development Program Focus Group Analysis

Notice that the comments from the focus group, shown in Table 7.8, were not thematically organized but just listed in the order they were spoken. These comments can be likened to "raw data" in that they have not been summarized or treated by the evaluator in any way. Notice also that the list of comments presents only the staff's comments to the first question. Much additional information was collected but has not been listed here. This is mentioned to remind the reader that only a fraction of the data summary work is included in the discussion.

The easiest way to make sense of the information is to conduct some type of content analysis. Evaluators have a number of choices in terms of the types of content analyses to select. An obvious first step would be to group similar comments together and identify emerging themes. Following this logic, it is often helpful to report the frequency with which respondents' comments supported identified themes. Another content analysis strategy is to weigh negative, positive, mixed, or neutral comments.

In all cases, replication of the emerging themes and content classifications is advisable. Having other evaluators conduct independent content analyses of the same information and subsequent comparison of results is an excellent strategy with which to establish objectivity of the content analysis. Barring the availability of another evaluator, a client might assist in this process. Minimally,

Table 7.8   Question 1a Focus Group Comments:
Usefulness of the Application Process

- Though I didn't have to write it, I thought that it was really neat—one page and limited to that. Director who did write it had some trouble communicating with the foundation consultant. They played phone tag with messages about changes. Rushed timetable. (1Sa)
- The consultants helped. I loved the one-page summary. The program is such a blessing, so gentle and kind, don't ask you to overextend. (2Sa)
- Sounded pretty clear as a 3-year commitment. Unless something really went wrong, they would get some funding. Very nice balance. Checkpoints along the way of a 3-year process. Sense of commitment. (3Sa)
- New staff understanding the foundation and the staff of the foundation. (4Sa)
- Yes, they need to be up front about what they really wanted. (1Sa)
- We understood the granting process more. (5Sa)
- The application process was hard work, but when done it was very, very valuable.
  It is a duplication, however, of a work plan developed earlier. (6Sa)
- The rewrites were good for us. It made us reflect on ourselves. (7Sa)
- Initially more confused than informed. Did not realize that their proposed activities were not community development until they talked with foundation consultant. (1Sb)
- Turned down flat the first time. Didn't really understand the difference between community development and program until yesterday. (2Sb)
- The staff need to be more up front with language and mission. (3Sb)
- It was complicated. (4Sb)
- The foundation tries to force a clear separation between community development and program when within some organizations this distinction is not clearly drawn. More respect for this would be welcome. (5Sb)
- I agree, a clearer explanation of what community development is with examples would be very helpful. (3Sb)
- Board's view of community development would have helped the groups. (6Sb)
- The staff needs to use examples from community development, not program. Why emphasize program, if you want community development? They need to make better connections between community development and program development. Can you always separate them? (7Sb)
- Loved the 4-column Learning and Evaluation form. [Another person agreed.] It might even replace the application form, because the L and E form clearly demonstrates that the development staff person cannot just put the application together. It forces the organization as a whole to think about the community development process. Might merge better the application with the L and E form. (8Sb)
- The application created frustration beyond any frustration ever encountered before in grant writing from someone who thinks of grant writing skills as a strength. The Learning and Evaluation form was beyond my capacity to figure out. Language was confusing, needs to be rewritten in simpler language. (9Sb)

the evaluator should attempt the categorization at least twice, with sufficient time in between to merit the determination of a second, independent trial.

Shown in Table 7.9 is the first attempt at grouping responses by theme. The evaluator went through the list of comments and identified preliminary themes. Notice that some theme headings have multiple comments listed and others have but one. The next step in this process is to combine themes where possible.

Table 7.9   Initial Analysis of Comments by Theme

Communication, understanding the foundation, the grant process

- Trouble communicating with foundation consultant. (1Sa)
- Yes, they need to be up front about what they really want. (1Sa)
- New staff understanding the foundation and the staff of the foundation. (4Sa)
- The staff need to be more up front with language and mission. (3Sb)
- We understood the granting process more. (5Sa)

Understanding community development

- Initially more confused than informed. Did not realize that their proposed activities were not community development until they talked with foundation consultant. (1Sb)
- Turned down flat the first time. Didn't really understand the difference between community development and program until yesterday. (2Sb)
- The foundation tries to force a clear separation between community development and program when within some organizations this distinction is not clearly drawn. More respect for this would be welcome. (5Sb)
- I agree, a clearer explanation of what community development is, with examples, would be very helpful. (3Sb)
- Board's view of community development would have helped the groups. (6Sb)
- The staff needs to use examples from community development, not program. Why emphasize program, if you want community development? They need to make better connections between community development and program development. Can you always separate them? (7Sb)

Hard work and complex effort

- The application process was hard work, but when done it was very, very valuable. (6Sa)
- It was complicated. (4Sb)

Duplication of effort

- It is a duplication, however, of a work plan developed earlier. (6Sa)

Time

- Rushed timetable (1Sa)

(Continued)

Table 7.9 (Continued)

Page length of application

- Really neat—one page and limited to that (1Sa)
- I loved one-page summary (2Sa)

Foundation consultants

- The consultants helped. (2Sa)

Promoted reflection

- The rewrites were good for us. It made us reflect on ourselves. (7Sa)

Learning and Evaluation form

- Loved the 4-column Learning and Evaluation form. [Another person agreed.] It might even replace the application form, because the L and E form clearly demonstrates that the development staff person cannot just put the application together. It forces the organization as a whole to think about the community development process. Might merge better the application with the L and E form. (8Sb)
- The application created frustration beyond any frustration ever encountered before in grant writing from someone who thinks of grant writing skills as a strength. The Learning and Evaluation form was beyond my capacity to figure out. Language was confusing, needs to be rewritten in simpler language. (9Sb)

Other

- Program is a blessing, so gentle and kind, don't ask you to overextend (2Sa)
- Sounded pretty clear as a 3-year commitment. Unless something really went wrong, they would get some funding. Very nice balance. Checkpoints along the way of a 3-year process. Sense of commitment. (3Sa)

Table 7.10 presents a revised version of the initial content analysis that has combined some of the initial themes under broader categories so that multiple, rather than single, comments are included. In essence, this process allows the evaluator to organize and summarize the information into progressively more meaningful segments. Certainly, understanding of community development already has emerged as the predominant theme of the focus group's comments, with communication with the foundation an obvious second.

Once the evaluator is satisfied with the analysis of the focus group data, the next step would be to communicate these findings to the appropriate audiences. The format of this communication varies by evaluation purpose and client. Choices available for reviewing evaluation findings and strategies for enhancing the collaborative nature of this activity are the subject of the next chapter.

Table 7.10   Revised Analysis of Comments by Theme

Understanding community development

- Initially more confused than informed. Did not realize that their proposed activities were not community development until they talked with foundation consultant. (1Sb)
- Turned down flat the first time. Didn't really understand the difference between community development and program until yesterday. (2Sb)
- The foundation tries to force a clear separation between community development and program when within some organizations this distinction is not clearly drawn. More respect for this would be welcome. (5Sb)
- I agree, a clearer explanation of what community development is, with examples, would be very helpful. (3Sb)
- Board's view of community development would have helped the groups. (6Sb)
- The staff need to use example from community development, not program. Why emphasize program, if you want community development? They need to make better connections between community development and program development. Can you always separate them? (7Sb)

Communication, understanding the foundation, the grant process

- Trouble communicating with foundation consultant. (1Sa)
- Yes, they need to be up front about what they really want. (1Sa)
- New staff understanding the foundation and the staff of the foundation. (4Sa)
- The staff need to be more up front with language and mission. (3Sb)
- We understood the granting process more. (5Sa)

Application preparation

- The application process was hard work, but when done it was very, very valuable. (6Sa)
- It was complicated. (4Sb)
- It is a duplication, however, of a work plan developed earlier. (6Sa)
- Rushed timetable (1Sa)
- Really neat—one page and limited to that (1Sa)
- I loved one-page summary (2Sa)

Learning and Evaluation form

- Loved the 4-column Learning and Evaluation form. [Another person agreed.] It might even replace the application form, because the L and E form clearly demonstrates that the development staff person cannot just put the application together. It forces the organization as a whole to think about the community development process. Might merge better the application with the L and E form. (8Sb)

(Continued)

Table 7.10 (Continued)

- The application created frustration beyond any frustration ever encountered before in grant writing from someone who thinks of grant writing skills as a strength. The Learning and Evaluation form was beyond my capacity to figure out. Language was confusing, needs to be rewritten in simpler language. (9Sb)

Other

- Program is a blessing, so gentle and kind, don't ask you to overextend (2Sa)
- Sounded pretty clear as a 3-year commitment. Unless something really went wrong, they would get some funding. Very nice balance. Checkpoints along the way of a 3-year process. Sense of commitment. (3Sa)
- The rewrites were good for us. It made us reflect on ourselves. (7Sa)
- The consultants helped. (2Sa)

Summary of Chapter Contents

This chapter examined quantitative and qualitative data analysis approaches in an effort to promote common language around the analysis part of an evaluation. The most common methods of both were presented and explained. The chapter briefly discussed the use of computer software to assist with both types of analyses. The section that followed provided examples of how collaborative evaluators engage stakeholders in summarizing the information gathered to answer evaluation questions. The Rural Economic Development Program was used as an example to demonstrate the application of data analysis within an evaluation context.

Chapter 7 Exercises

TEFLEP SECOND PREGNANCY DATA

Recall that for the TEFLEP program, 36 of the 151 teen participants became pregnant during the 3-year program. The control group was dropped from the evaluation, as only 18 of the original 35 completed the study assessments. Although the evaluator could have used teen second pregnancy statistics for the region, she decided that evidence from an equivalent comparison group (Smith & Glass, 1987) would provide stronger evidence to probe the more important intended outcomes of the study. As teens usually gave birth for the first time in the local hospital, the evaluator could identify all teens who gave birth the year before TEFLEP began. From that list, 50 first-time teen mothers were randomly selected for interviews. Of those 50 identified, 35 were located and actually provided information.

Activity

Second pregnancy data for TEFLEP participants and the equivalent comparison group are provided in Table 7.11, with level of participation included for TEFLEP participants. Analyze these data in ways that address the effectiveness of the program at delaying second pregnancy and the possible influence of program participation on the delay.

Table 7.11   Second Pregnancy Data for TEFLEP Participants and Equivalent Comparison Group

ID No.	Treatment or Comparison Group	Number of Months Since Birth of First Child	Level of TEFLEP Activities[a]
7	T	8	L
9	T	14	L
10	T	17	M
12	T	19	H
17	T	9	L
21	T	13	H
24	T	21	H
28	T	15	M
29	T	24	H
30	T	16	M

(Continued)

Table 7.11 (Continued)

ID No.	Treatment or Comparison Group	Number of Months Since Birth of First Child	Level of TEFLEP Activities[a]
33	T	22	H
36	T	28	H
39	T	18	M
43	T	8	L
47	T	14	M
49	T	20	M
51	T	18	M
54	T	21	H
58	T	17	H
61	T	16	M
62	T	23	H
66	T	15	L
67	T	23	H
70	T	9	L
72	T	13	M
79	T	8	L
83	T	14	M
84	T	22	H
88	T	12	M
90	T	16	M
93	T	15	L
98	T	10	M
101	T	14	M
109	T	17	H
111	T	13	M
123	T	9	M
152	C	17	
155	C	8	
156	C	11	
159	C	14	
160	C	9	
161	C	12	
163	C	11	
164	C	13	
166	C	22	
169	C	9	
171	C	13	
173	C	12	
177	C	9	
179	C	18	
180	C	8	

a. H = high, M = medium, L = low.

DATA FROM TEFLEP MOTHERS OF TEENS

The comments that follow were received from a random sample of mothers whose daughters participated in the TEFLEP program. They were responding to the question, "What one thing would you say to a friend whose daughter is thinking about joining the TEFLEP program?"

Activity

Analyze the data listed here, organizing responses by theme.

1. My daughter went to almost all the meetings.

2. I liked the way the girls got to participate in the crafts cooperative.

3. Even though my daughter went to the meetings, she got pregnant again.

4. I thought TEFLEP would help her get a good job, but it didn't.

5. I was delighted that the program helped my daughter complete two of her G-level exams.

6. It's good that the girls have some place to go after they get pregnant. The counselors talk to them and they listen.

7. TEFLEP week on the island was a lot of fun for the girls.

8. My daughter went back to school with the help of TEFLEP.

9. The sale of crafts brought some money into the house.

10. My daughter learned how to make and sell crafts.

11. My daughter likes to go to meetings. She's very glad she's in the program.

12. After my daughter joined TEFLEP, I let her and the baby move back in with me. She needs to go back to school.

13. If you want your daughter to get family planning, the TEFLEP clinic will do that.

14. The crafts counselor taught the girls good skills and they had a good time.

15. Joining TEFLEP was good for my daughter. It helped her see that she had choices.

16. I think the girls shouldn't get pregnant in the first place.

17. The fathers never really participated in the program. My daughter broke up with him soon after the baby was born.

18. When your daughter is in TEFLEP, she has someone to talk with about her problems.

19. Even though my daughter used family planning, she got pregnant again.

20. TEFLEP can help girls not get pregnant again.

21. The people in the program came to visit my daughter every 6 months at home.

22. My daughter has turned her life around; your daughter can do it too.

23. My daughter doesn't tell me much about TEFLEP.

TEFLEP COMMUNITY AWARENESS SURVEY RESULTS

Table 7.12 shows the results of a community awareness survey, done to determine what the community knew about TEFLEP. Two data collectors were sent to the central market on a Saturday morning when it was busiest. Survey participants were asked their occupation; whether they had heard of TEFLEP; and if they had heard of it, what they thought the strength of the program was. Data collectors were instructed to continue asking people this question until they had questioned 20 people who had heard of the program.

Activity

Using the data in Table 7.12, summarize the information and the responses to the question, "Was TEFLEP a well-known program in the community?

Table 7.12   TEFLEP Community Awareness Survey Results

No.	Occupation	Gender	Heard of TEFLEP	Strength of TEFLEP
1	Clerk	M	Y	I bought some key chains the girls made
2	Teacher	M	Y	They have a week of special activities
3	Secretary	F	N	
4	Laborer	F	N	
5	Factory worker	M	N	
6	Clerk	F	Y	Girls shouldn't get pregnant again
7	Domestic	F	Y	TEFLEP girls are proud of the program

Table 7.12 (continued)

No.	Occupation	Gender	Heard of TEFLEP	Strength of TEFLEP
8	Teacher	F	N	
9	Nurse	F	Y	Helps them find jobs
10	Clerk	M	Y	Not sure
11	Factory worker	M	N	
12	Housewife	F	Y	Don't know
13	Instructor	M	Y	Keeps teens from getting pregnant again
14	Salesperson	F	N	
15	Housewife	F	Y	Teen mothers learn crafts to earn money
16	Teacher	M	N	
17	Clerk	F	Y	Prevents them from idling
18	Clerk	M	Y	Can't say
19	Domestic	F	N	
20	Mechanic	M	Y	Don't really know
21	Secretary	F	Y	Prevent unwanted pregnancies
22	Housewife	F	N	
23	Salesperson	M	Y	Don't know
24	Clerk	M	Y	Teen mothers don't lose hope
25	Driver	M	N	
26	Laborer	M	Y	Finds the girls jobs
27	Domestic	F	Y	Tells girls to wait to have their next baby
28	Mechanic	M	N	
29	Factory worker	F	Y	Some girls can continue their education
30	Doctor's assistant	F	Y	Heard about activities on the radio
31	Clerk	F	N	
32	Housewife	F	N	
33	Secretary	M	Y	Girls can go back to school
34	Clerk	M	N	
35	Domestic	F	Y	Allows girls to plan their families

8

Collaborative
Review of Findings

J ust as data collection and analysis can be done collaboratively, summarizing and reviewing evaluation findings can be done in ways that engage stakeholders in the process. Of all the steps in a program evaluation, review of the findings can be the most problematic, as the choices are many and the complexity is great. A collaborative stance can facilitate the process, which will promote the ultimate purpose of most evaluations: to provide useful information about the program.

This chapter discusses how review of evaluation findings fits within the evaluation process. It also presents alternative formats for facilitating that review, emphasizing the importance of intended audiences. Additionally, the chapter suggests ways in which the review process can be organized to allow opportunities for stakeholder participation. Finally, examples are offered of how an evaluator might review findings for the two data analysis situations in chapter 7.

Review of Evaluation Findings:
The Final Evaluation Step

Evaluation efforts culminate in the review of evaluation findings. The reasons behind clarifying the evaluation, developing a viable evaluation plan, and implementing that plan by collecting and summarizing information come to fruition when the evaluation findings are reviewed. Without a review of the findings, the other efforts of the evaluation are virtually meaningless.

With many evaluations, sharing findings is sequentially the final evaluation event. Figure 8.1 depicts this linear sequence.

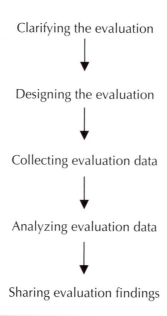

Clarifying the evaluation

Designing the evaluation

Collecting evaluation data

Analyzing evaluation data

Sharing evaluation findings

Figure 8.1   Linear Model of Sharing Collaborative Evaluation Findings

In this model, the sharing of evaluation findings occurs across all data collection activities, usually in a written evaluation report at the end of the evaluation.

Another model for sharing evaluation findings conceptualizes it as iterative with data collection efforts. As shown in Figure 8.2, after clarification of the evaluation and evaluation planning, each data collection activity has an information-sharing event attached to it. For example, if the evaluation called for a focus group of participants, the findings of that focus group would be shared with program staff as soon as they were available. The evaluator would not wait for the end of the evaluation to share the results.

One advantage of the iterative model is that information is provided to program staff in a timely fashion. It would not make a great deal of sense to wait to share information that could lead immediately to program improvement. Another advantage of the iterative model is that program stakeholders are aware of findings early so that adjustments can be made to the overall evaluation design if necessary. For example, evaluator site visit interviews might determine that program implementation had fallen behind schedule. With this information, program staff and evaluators might decide to delay collection of interim survey data until more implementation progress had been made.

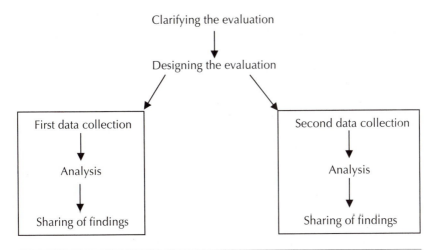

Figure 8.2   Iterative Model of Sharing Collaborative Evaluation Findings

Often, a combination of the two models is adopted. Following this mixed-model approach, evaluators share findings when available and then integrate all findings in a final evaluation report. The value of sharing findings in final evaluation reports, however, has been questioned (Patton, 1997). Those commissioning the evaluation often decide they need a final report without carefully reflecting about the value of such a report. Any number of final evaluation reports have waited, unread and gathering dust on many a shelf. The resources involved in generating them might better have been directed into a superior quality of data collection and analysis.

Independent of the decision to create some type of final report, evaluators must communicate evaluation findings in a timely fashion. Nothing in a final evaluation report should be a surprise to program staff. Staff should be involved in the evaluation process such that preliminary findings are shared and program staff members have had an opportunity to probe them with the evaluator. This is not to say that evaluators are obligated to adjust their findings to please program staff. Quite the contrary—evaluators are bound by professional practice guidelines to provide fair and complete findings. The sharing of findings helps both program staff and evaluators interpret the meaning of the findings.

Alternative Formats

Although sharing evaluation findings most often occurs through written interim and final evaluation reports, a host of other reporting options are available.

Both the method of reporting and the frequency of reporting are subject to negotiation between the program and the evaluator. Additionally, the audiences for whom the evaluation is intended may vary and should be specified before the evaluation is performed. Collaborative evaluators communicate with stakeholders about the available options. Stakeholders in turn must share with evaluators their reporting needs. Together they forge a plan for reporting.

CHOICES IN METHOD OF REPORTING

Evaluation reports can take many forms. They may differ by medium (e.g., written, oral, video) and level of formality (i.e., very formal to very informal). They also may vary by level of technical detail.

Methods of Sharing Findings

Typically, evaluators share their findings using written reports, but other media are growing in popularity. The following are commonly considered for sharing evaluation findings.

Interim Evaluation Reports. This option is usually written and summarizes findings for a specified time within the overall evaluation period. It usually chronicles evaluation efforts and contains the results of separate data collection efforts.

Summary Evaluation Report. This also can be called the final evaluation report. Typically, it contains the answers to crosswalk evaluation questions, with multiple data sources summarized for each question.

Executive Summary. This report is often added to lengthy evaluation reports to provide readers with quick access to the report's contents. Normally, this report will summarize key evaluation findings.

Press Release. This document is prepared from the evaluation report, usually by public relations or media specialists within the program. This format invites newspapers and magazines to cover the evaluation findings.

Web Postings. Excerpts from evaluation reports, summaries of findings, and press releases may be posted on program websites to enable a wide audience to view evaluation findings.

Monographs. These documents are prepared for dissemination to wide audiences, usually with the intention of sharing lessons learned.

Portfolios. This collection of program artifacts and reports is compiled to represent what has occurred in the program. By viewing primary program and evaluation documents, those interested can gain insight into the program.

Videos and PowerPoint Presentations. These strategies are finding growing favor among many who are interested in depicting program events and accomplishments because they are readily understood by most audiences and can be very persuasive.

Level of Formality

All media selected for sharing evaluation findings may be prepared in either a formal or informal manner. For example, an interim evaluation report might be in the form of a quick memo or oral report; on the other hand, it could translate into a 200-page document. The level of formality needs to be negotiated between the evaluator and the client. If at all possible, it should be part of the initial contract negotiation, as more formal reporting takes more resources to produce than does less formal reporting.

Technical Detail

Whatever the degree of formality used or the medium selected to share evaluation findings, the technical details of the evaluation should always be well documented. Evaluators must keep complete records about decisions made concerning sampling, instrument development, and data analysis. A paper trail should exist so that a third party could recreate what was done and achieve similar results. This is to say that the elements of a completed evaluation's technical report should be on file, if they are not enclosed with the final report.

CHOICES IN FREQUENCY OF REPORTING

Frequency of reporting is another dynamic to consider when determining the method of sharing findings. Ideally, whenever findings are available, they should be shared as soon as possible. Within that guideline, the nature of the evaluation will shape the number of needed contacts. Complicated evaluations with multiple embedded decision points will require more frequent sharing of findings than less complex endeavors. Frequency of reporting also will be determined by the size and scope of the evaluation and the agency sponsoring it. Although exceptions exist, larger evaluations usually require more frequent communication about findings than smaller evaluations. Larger organizations may require that evaluation findings be shared among different subgroups within the organization, which would require more frequent meetings about findings.

AUDIENCE IDENTIFICATION

Evaluations normally have multiple audiences interested in the findings. Program sponsors, governing boards, program staff, participants, and the public comprise the more common stakeholders who might be interested in evaluation findings. These groups require different types of information in differing formats. Thus, evaluators need to consider which of these audiences will need information. The actual decision will be guided almost exclusively by who is commissioning the evaluation. If possible, the evaluator should determine with the client at the contract stage how many audiences require information about evaluation findings.

Opportunities for Collaboration With Review of Findings

Stakeholders can be engaged in the review of findings by (a) asking them to assist with data interpretation, (b) providing them with drafts of evaluation reports for comment, and (c) making sure that they understand the information presented. This engagement can help stakeholders acquire important insights into the findings. It also allows for concerns about the findings to surface early. Finally, engagement in the process will permit the intended audience to better understand the findings.

At times, in their distance from a program, evaluators will find out about aspects of a program and will not necessarily be able to interpret the findings. During the TEFLEP evaluation, the evaluator discovered that ten of the 11 teen participants who had lost their babies in miscarriages or birth complications were among those who became pregnant for a second time during the program. Initially, the evaluator thought that this indicated that these teens had intended to become pregnant in the first place. After consultation with the program staff, she found out it was the sense of loss that spurred these teens to become pregnant a second time.

Draft reports are an excellent way of engaging stakeholders in the review of findings. This method more than any other will communicate to the evaluator the degree to which the reported findings and format are consistent with the sponsor's expectations. Often, sponsors are unaware of how evaluation findings will be represented. It is only when they see or hear about the findings that they can make a determination about the level of acceptability. This has nothing to do with the content, nor does it imply that evaluators should change results should the client not like them. It has more to do with how the results are communicated and a matching of expectations with format. Additionally, when evaluators label reports as drafts, it communicates to clients a genuine desire to have the findings address mutually important issues.

Finally, sharing results with stakeholders allows the evaluator to determine the extent to which findings are understood. On occasion, presentations of findings are not geared to the technical competence of the audience. When the evaluator engages stakeholders in the review of findings, mismatches can be bridged to promote better understanding.

Quantitative Example: The Rural Economic Development Program

Recall that in chapter 6, the evaluator for the Rural Economic Development Program used an annual survey of grantees to gather some of the information to answer the question: "In what ways have grantees enhanced existing organizational networks?" All 10 grantees responded about the difference in their collaboration from Year 1 of the program to Year 2, addressing three different types of collaboration: making referrals, receiving referrals, and working together toward a common goal. The evaluator analyzed the data, providing means, standard deviations, and t statistics for the three types of collaboration. Further, the evaluator went on to calculate effect sizes for the three types of collaboration. The questions relevant at this juncture are, What should be shared? and What form should that sharing take?

Although some general guidelines apply, the specifics of the evaluation will determine many of the answers to these questions. Ordinarily, the actual data summarized by individuals or, in this case, grantees is not shared. Rather, a summary form of it is shared. Table 8.1 contains ranges of responses, means, standard deviations, effect sizes, and t statistics, with probabilities for Year 1 and Year 2. If a table like Table 8.1 is included in the review of findings, a written explanation of the table should accompany it. The purpose of a table is to assist the reader in making sense of the information. The narrator's task is to make sure that the highlights of the table are emphasized in the text. For example, a narration of Table 8.1 might read as follows:

> Data in Table 8.1 show increases in collaboration from Year 1 to Year 2 across all three types of collaboration. Effect size calculations reveal strongest increases for the numbers of organizations to which grantees make referrals, as well as those from which they receive referrals. These increases were statistically significant for making referrals ($t = 5.03, p < .001$) and receiving referrals ($t = 2.91, p < .017$) but not for working together toward a common goal.

This narration would be appropriate for a sophisticated research audience but would not do well as a press release. Having the data analysis to support statements about programs is essential, but sharing all the analysis details is not

Table 8.1   Cohort 1 Collaboration by Type of Collaboration, Years 1 and 2

Types of Collaboration Cohort 1 (n = 10 grantees)	End Year 1	End Year 2	Effect Size	t (Probability)
Make referrals to				
Mean	8	9.6	+.34	5.03 (.001)
(SD)	(5.03)	(4.40)		
Response range	0–16	0–15		
Receive referrals from				
Mean	7.7	9.8	+.3.5	2.91 (.017)
(SD)	(5.23)	(6.83)		
Response range	0–18	0–22		
Work together toward common goal				
Mean	4.2	4.7	+.16	1.63 (.138)
(SD)	(3.43)	(2.91)		
Response range	0–10	2–10		

Note: SD = standard deviation.

necessarily helpful. Evaluators must conduct the strongest analyses possible and then decide how much detail is useful for the audience's understanding.

In this case, the evaluator met with the Rural Economic Development Program staff and shared a draft of the technical report summary. Together they reviewed findings, staff asked questions, and then they discussed the level of information that was needed for the upcoming meeting of the board of directors.

Qualitative Example: The Rural Economic Development Program

The evaluator's task, once the data from the Rural Economic Development Program focus group meetings have been analyzed, is to summarize these comments so that the audience can make sense of the information. Most focus group summaries should include sections on the purpose of the focus group, sample selection, and instrument development (including a sample of the protocol), as well as a summary of the results. The evaluator might decide to include a list of all comments or transcriptions as an optional appendix.

Table 8.2   Revised Organization of Comments by Theme

Understanding community development
- Initially more confused than informed. Did not realize that their proposed activities were not community development until they talked with foundation consultant. (1Sb)
- Turned down flat the first time. Didn't really understand the difference between community development and program until yesterday. (2Sb)
- The foundation tries to force a clear separation between community development and program when within some organizations this distinction is not clearly drawn. More respect for this would be welcome. (5Sb)
- I agree, a clearer explanation of what community development is, with examples, would be very helpful. (3Sb)
- Board's view of community development would have helped the groups. (6Sb)
- The staff needs to use examples from community development, not program. Why emphasize program, if you want community development? They need to make better connections between community development and program development. Can you always separate them? (7Sb)

Communication, understanding the foundation, the grant process
- Trouble communicating with foundation consultant. (1Sa)
- Yes, they need to be up front about what they really wanted. (1Sa)
- New staff understanding the foundation and the staff of the foundation. (4Sa)
- The staff needs to be more up front with language and mission. (3Sb)
- We understood the granting process more. (5Sa)

Application preparation
- The application process was hard work but when done it was very, very valuable. (6Sa)
- It was complicated. (4Sb)
- It is a duplication, however, of a work plan developed earlier. (6Sa)
- Rushed timetable (1Sa)
- Really neat—one page and limited to that (1Sa)
- I loved one-page summary (2Sa)

Learning and Evaluation form
- Loved the 4-column Learning and Evaluation form. [Another person agreed.] It might even replace the application form, because the L and E form clearly demonstrates that the development staff person cannot just put the application together. It forces the organization as a whole to think about the community development process. Might merge better the application with the L and E form. (8Sb)
- The application created frustration beyond any frustration ever encountered before in grant writing from someone who thinks of grant writing skills as a strength. The Learning and Evaluation form was beyond my capacity to figure out. Language was confusing, needs to be rewritten in simpler language. (9Sb)

(Continued)

Table 8.2 (Continued)

Other

- Program is a blessing, so gentle and kind, don't ask you to overextend (2Sa)
- Sounded pretty clear as a 3-year commitment. Unless something really went wrong, they would get some funding. Very nice balance. Checkpoints along the way of a 3-year process. Sense of commitment. (3Sa)
- The rewrites were good for us. It made us reflect on ourselves. (7Sa)
- The consultants helped. (2Sa)

Table 8.2 presents a revised version of the initial content analysis that has combined some of the initial themes under broader categories so that multiple, rather than single, comments are included. In essence, this process allows the evaluator to organize and summarize the information into progressively more meaningful segments. Certainly, understanding of community development already has emerged as the predominant theme of the focus group comments, with communication with the foundation an obvious second.

Notice that the original 10 categories have been reduced to 5. This will make narration of the data easier. The evaluator should always narrate the contents of a table to assist the reader's understanding. The purpose of the narration is to guide the reader through the table and point out noteworthy information. The narration further allows the evaluator to interpret the information in the table. Tables should contain digestible portions of information. Ideally, tables should not exceed a page in length.

The actual focus group report summary for the information contained in Table 8.2 is presented in Figure 8.3. The evaluator begins the summary by commenting on the overall nature of the comments. Note that subsequently the evaluator has dismantled the table and included the comments after each section of the focus group summary, corresponding to the five themes identified. This allows the reader to consider the themes individually.

The evaluator would then take the remaining information question by question, analyzing and reporting data in a similar fashion. With greater numbers of focus group participants, the summary strategy would probably require additional steps in the analysis. Rather than individual comments, themes are reported with the numbers of comments contained within each of the themes. Examples of comments may be included to provide the reader with a flavor of the type of comments included in the theme category.

Staff Views: Question 1a—Usefulness of the Application

Overall, regarding the first question about the usefulness of the application, 6 of the 18 participants focused on their need to have the foundation better define community development. Five organizations spoke about the importance of communication with the foundation, and six organizations commented on the application process. Two comments about the Learning and Evaluation form shared very divergent perspectives, and four comments were unique to individual organizations. Among the comments, seven were generally positive, one expressed extreme frustration with the process, one observed that the application process was complicated, and the remaining nine made suggestions for improvement.

Understanding Community Development

Six organizations commented that the foundation needs to better define the content and scope of community development. Five of the six expressly focused on confusion between program development and community development as defined by the foundation. Focus group comments about this theme are presented here.

- Initially more confused than informed. Did not realize that their proposed activities were not community development until they talked with foundation consultant. (1Sb)
- Turned down flat the first time. Didn't really understand the difference between community development and program until yesterday. (2Sb)
- The foundation tries to force a clear separation between community development and program when within some organizations this distinction is not clearly drawn. More respect for this would be welcome. (5Sb)
- I agree, a clearer explanation of what community development is with examples would be very helpful. (3Sb)
- Board's view of community development would have helped the groups. (6Sb)
- The staff need to use example from community development, not program. Why emphasize program, if you want community development? They need to make better connections between community development and program development. Can you always separate them? (7Sb)

Communication, Understanding the Foundation, the Grant Process
Another set of comments addressed the need for better communication between applicants and the foundation. One of these comments, "Yes, they need to be up front about what they really wanted," might be linked to the previous theme that identified confusion about the distinction between program development and community development. Here are the remaining comments.

- Trouble communicating with foundation consultant. (1Sa)
- New staff understanding the foundation and the staff of the foundation. (4Sa)
- The staff need to be more up front with language and mission. (3Sb)
- We understood the granting process more. (5Sa)

Figure 8.3   Rural Economic Development Focus Group Summary

Figure 8.3 (Continued)

Application Preparation
Three staff participants in the focus group were complimentary of the application process.

- Really neat—one page and limited to that (1Sa)
- I loved one-page summary (2Sa)
- The application process was hard work but when done it was very, very valuable. (6Sa)

The remaining three comments expressed concern.

- It was complicated. (4Sb)
- It is a duplication, however, of a work plan developed earlier. (6Sa)
- Rushed timetable (1Sa)

Learning and Evaluation Form
The Learning and Evaluation form used by the foundation was viewed very differently by two of the staff members during the focus groups. One person was very complimentary:

- Loved the 4-column Learning and Evaluation form. [Another person agreed.] It might even replace the application form, because the L and E form clearly demonstrates that the development staff person cannot just put the application together. It forces the organization as a whole to think about the community development process. Might merge better the application with the L and E form. (8Sb)

Another focus group participant expressed frustration in an equivalently strong manner:

- The application created frustration beyond any frustration ever encountered before in grant writing from someone who thinks of grant writing skills as a strength. The Learning and Evaluation form was beyond my capacity to figure out. Language was confusing, needs to be rewritten in simpler language. (9Sb)

Other
Finally, four focus group participants had observations about the focus group process that were different from any of the previously identified themes.
- Program is a blessing, so gentle and kind, don't ask you to overextend (2Sa)
- Sounded pretty clear as a 3-year commitment. Unless something really went wrong, they would get some funding. Very nice balance. Checkpoints along the way of a 3-year process. Sense of commitment. (3Sa)
- The rewrites were good for us. It made us reflect on ourselves. (7Sa)
- The consultants helped. (2Sa)

Summary of Chapter Contents

This chapter reviewed how reporting evaluation findings fits within the overall evaluation context and suggested alternatives that are available. Collaborative evaluation stresses the importance of engaging stakeholders in the selection of desired evaluation formats but acknowledges that in terms of reporting, stakeholders may need examples before they can decide on what they want. Engaging them in the review of draft reports can facilitate this process. Finally, this chapter provides an example of an evaluator-prepared report for stakeholder review, using the two data analysis examples from chapter 7.

Chapter 8 Exercises

Activity

From the data analyzed at the end of chapter 7, create reports for the following.

1. TEFLEP Second Pregnancy Data

2. Data from TEFLEP mothers of teens

3. TEFLEP Community Awareness Survey results

References

American Evaluation Association. (1995). Guiding principles for evaluators. *New Directions for Program Evaluation, 34,* 19-26.

Barley, A. L., & Jenness, M. (1993). Cluster evaluation: A method to strengthen evaluation in smaller programs with similar purposes. *Evaluation Practice, 14*(2), 141-147.

Bloom, B. S. (Ed.). (1956). *Taxonomy of educational objectives: The classification of educational goals. Handbook I: Cognitive domain.* New York: Longmans.

Brandon, P. R. (1998). Stakeholder participation for the purpose of helping ensure evaluation validity: Bridging the gap between collaborative and non-collaborative evaluations. *American Journal of Evaluation, 19*(3), 325-353.

Brunner, I., & Guzman, A. (1989). Participatory evaluation: A tool to assess projects and empower people. In F. R. Connor & M. H. Hendricks (Eds.), *New directions for program evaluation, 42,* 9-17.

Burke, B. (1998). Evaluation for a change: Reflections on participatory methodology. *New Directions for Program Evaluation, 80,* 43-56.

Callaway, S., Arnold, M., & Norman, P. (Eds.). (1993). *Community voices: Leadership development for community decision-making: Program implementation guide.* Greensboro, NC: Cooperative Extension Program, North Carolina Agricultural and Technical State University.

Campbell, D. T., & Stanley, J. C. (1966). *Experimental and quasi-experimental designs for research.* Chicago: Rand McNally.

Chelimsky, E. (1986). What have we learned about the politics of program evaluation? *Evaluation Practice, 8*(1), 5-22.

Christie, C. A. (Ed.). (2003). The practice-theory relationship in evaluation. *New Directions for Evaluation, 97*(Special Issue).

Ciarlo, J. A. (Ed.). (1981). *Utilizing evaluation.* Beverly Hills, CA: Sage.

Cook, T. D., & Campbell, D. T. (1979). *Quasi-experimentation: Design and analysis issues for field settings.* Chicago: Rand McNally.

Coupal, F. P., & Simoneau, M. (1998). A case study of participatory evaluation in Haiti. *New Directions for Program Evaluation, 80,* 69-79.

Cousins, J. B., Donohue, J. J., & Bloom, G. A. (1996). Collaborative evaluation in North America: Evaluators' self-reported opinions, practices, and consequences. *Evaluation Practice, 17*(3), 207-226.

Cousins, J. B., & Earl. L. M. (1992). The case for participatory evaluation. *Educational Evaluation and Policy Analysis, 14*(4), 397-418.

Cousins, J. B., & Earl. L. M. (Eds.). (1995). *Participatory evaluation in education: Studies of evaluation use and organizational learning.* London: Falmer.

Cousins, J. B., & Whitmore, E. (1998). Framing participatory evaluation. *New Directions for Program Evaluation, 80,* 5-23.

Cronbach, L. J. (1963). Course improvement through evaluation. *Teachers College Record, 64*(8), 672-683.

Denzin, N. K., & Lincoln, Y. S. (Eds.). (2000). *Handbook of qualitative research* (2nd ed.). Thousand Oaks, CA: Sage.

Dillman, D. A. (1999). *Mail and Internet surveys: The tailored design method* (2nd ed.). New York: John Wiley.

Eisner, E. W. (1983). Education connoisseurship and criticism: Their form and functions in educational evaluation. In G. F. Madaus, E. L. Stufflebeam, & M. S. Scriven (Eds.), *Evaluation models: Viewpoints on educational and human services evaluation* (pp. 335-348). Boston, MA: Kluwer-Nijoff.

Eisner, E. W. (1991). *The enlightened eye.* New York: Macmillan.

Fetterman, D. M. (1994). Empowerment evaluation. *Evaluation Practice, 15*(1), 1-15.

Fetterman, D. M. (1995). In response to Dr. Daniel Stufflebeam's "Empowerment evaluation, objectivist evaluation, and evaluation standards: Where the future of evaluation should not go and where it needs to go." *Evaluation Practice, 16,* 179-199.

Fetterman, D. M. (2001). *Foundation of empowerment evaluation.* Thousand Oaks, CA: Sage.

Fetterman, D. M., Kaftarian, S. J., & Wandersman, A. (Eds.). (1996). *Empowerment evaluation.* Thousand Oaks, CA: Sage.

Gall, M. D., Gall, J. P., & Borg, W. R. (2003). *Educational research* (7th ed.). Boston, MA: Allyn & Bacon.

Gardner, H. (1983). *Frames of mind: The theory of multiple intelligences.* New York: Basic Books.

Gardner, H. (1999). *Intelligence reframed.* New York: Basic Books.

Gaventa, J., Creed, V., & Morrissey, J. (1998). Scaling up: Participatory monitoring and evaluation of a federal empowerment program. *New Directions for Program Evaluation, 80,* 81-94.

Goldman, B. A., & Mitchell, D. E. (1997). *Directory of unpublished and experimental measures* (Vol. 7). Dubuque, IA: William C Brown.

Greene, J. G. (1987). Stakeholder participation and utilization in program evaluation. *Evaluation Review, 12*(2), 91-116.

Gregorc, A. F. (1999). *Style delineator.* Columbia, CT: Gregorc Associates.

Guba, E. G., & Lincoln, Y. S. (1981). *Effective evaluation: Improving the usefulness of evaluation results through responsive and naturalistic approaches.* San Francisco: Jossey-Bass.

Guba, E. G., & Lincoln, Y. S. (1989). *Fourth generation evaluation.* Newbury Park, CA: Sage.

Henry, G. (1990). *Practical sampling.* Thousand Oaks, CA: Sage.

Henry, R. (1992, November). *A delicate balance: The role of the cluster evaluator in relation to the foundation project directors.* Paper presented at the annual meeting of the American Evaluation Association, Seattle, WA.

House, E. R. (1978, March). Assumptions underlying evaluation models. *Educational Researcher,* pp. 4-11.

Jaeger, R. M. (1984). *Sampling in education and the social sciences.* New York: Longman.

Jaeger, R. M., O'Sullivan, R. G., Hecht, K. A., House, E. R., & Stake, R. E. (1986). Modular design for an evaluation of the Close Up Foundation programs. Greensboro, NC: Center for Educational Research and Evaluation, School of Education, University of North Carolina, Greensboro.

Jenness, M., & Barley, Z. A. (1992, November). *A constructivist approach to cluster evaluation.* Paper presented at the annual meeting of the American Evaluation Association, Seattle, WA.

Joint Committee on Standards for Educational Evaluation. (1994). *The program evaluation standards.* Thousand Oaks, CA: Sage.

Kellogg Foundation. (1991). *Information on cluster evaluation.* Battlecreek, MI: Author.

King, J. A. (1998). Making sense of participatory evaluation practice. *New Directions for Program Evaluation, 80,* 57-67.

Knott, T. D. (1988). The impact of major consumer groups on health care evaluation. *New Directions for Program Evaluation, 39,* 33-46.

Kraemer, H. C., & Thiemann, S. (1987). *How many subjects? Statistical power analysis in research.* Newbury Park, CA: Sage.

Krueger, R. A., & Casey, M. A. (2000). *Focus groups.* Thousand Oaks, CA: Sage.

Levin, H. M. (1996). Empowerment evaluation and accelerated schools. In D. M. Fetterman, S. J. Kaftarian, & A. Wandersman (Eds.), *Empowerment evaluation: Knowledge and tools for self-assessment and accountability.* Thousand Oaks, CA: Sage.

Lincoln, Y. S., & Guba, E. G. (1985). *Naturalistic inquiry.* Beverly Hills, CA: Sage.

Linney, J. A., & Wandersman, A. (1996). Empowering community groups with evaluation skills: The Prevention Plus III Model. In D. M. Fetterman, S. J. Kaftarian, & A. Wandersman (Eds.), *Empowerment evaluation: Knowledge and tools for self-assessment and accountability.* Thousand Oaks, CA: Sage.

Mansberger, N. B. (1993, November). *Making sense out of a mixed bag of data: The use of working hypotheses.* Paper presented at the annual meeting of the American Evaluation Association, Dallas, TX.

Miles, M. B., & Huberman, A. M. (1994). *Qualitative data analysis* (2nd ed.). Thousand Oaks, CA: Sage.

Mowbray, C. T. (1988). Getting the system to respond to evaluation findings. *New Directions for Program Evaluation, 39,* 47-58.

O'Sullivan, R. G. (1984). *Evaluation in developing countries: A case study of the St. Kitts Teenage Family Life Education Program.* Unpublished doctoral dissertation, Auburn University, Alabama.

O'Sullivan, R. G. (1991). Improving evaluation design and use through the "evaluation crosswalk" method. *National Forum of Applied Education Research Journal, 4,* 43-49.

O'Sullivan, R. G. (1995). From judges to collaborators: Evaluators' role in science curriculum reform. *New Directions for Program Evaluation, 65,* 19-30.

O'Sullivan, R. G. (1999a, April). *Evaluating school to work: A collaborative approach.* Paper presented at the annual meeting of the American Educational Research Association, Orlando, FL.

O'Sullivan, R. G. (1999b). From responsive to collaborative evaluation. In *Proceedings of the 1998 Stake Symposium on Evaluation.* Champaign-Urbana, IL: Center for Instructional Research and Curriculum Evaluation, University of Illinois.

O'Sullivan, R. G., Clinton, J., Schmidt-Davis, H., & Wall, S. (1996). *First year smart start evaluation of the Forsyth Early Childhood Partnership.* Greensboro, NC: Teaching to Diversity, University of North Carolina, Greensboro.

O'Sullivan, R. G., & D'Agostino, A. (1998, November). *How collaborative approaches promote evaluation with community-based programs for young children and their families.* Paper presented at the annual meeting of the American Evaluation Association, Chicago.

O'Sullivan, R. G., & D'Agostino, A. (2002). Promoting evaluation through collaboration: Findings from community-based programs for young children and their families. *Evaluation, 8*(3), 372-387.

O'Sullivan, R. G., D'Agostino, A., Prohm, B., Roche, L., & Schmidt-Davis, H. (1997). *1997 annual evaluation report of the Forsyth Early Childhood Partnership.* Greensboro, NC: Teaching to Diversity, University of North Carolina at Greensboro.

O'Sullivan, R. G., Adams, A., Ashburn, C., Blaisdell, B., Blake, L., Chernow, M., et al. (2002, March). *Cognitive styles and research orientation.* Paper presented at the annual meeting of the North Carolina Association for Research in Education, Chapel Hill, NC.

O'Sullivan, R. G., & O'Sullivan, J. M. (1994, May). *Evaluation voices: Promoting cluster evaluation from within programs.* Paper presented at the annual meeting of the Canadian Evaluation Society, Quebec City, Quebec.

O'Sullivan, R. G., & O'Sullivan, J. M. (1998). Evaluation voices: Promoting evaluation from within programs through collaboration. *Evaluation and Program Planning, 21*(1), 21-29.

Patton, M. Q. (1986). *Utilization-focused evaluation* (2nd ed.). Beverly Hills, CA: Sage.

Patton, M. Q. (1988). Integrating evaluation into a program for increased utility and cost-effectiveness. *New Directions for Program Evaluation, 39,* 85-94.

Patton, M. Q. (1990). *Qualitative evaluation and research methods* (2nd ed.). Newbury Park, CA: Sage.

Patton, M. Q. (1997). *Utilization-focused evaluation* (3rd ed.). Thousand Oaks, CA: Sage.

Patton, M. Q. (2002). *Qualitative research and evaluation methods* (3rd ed.). Thousand Oaks, CA: Sage.

Pearl, J. B., & Rubino, A. (1993, November). *The power of cluster evaluation networking conferences.* Paper presented at the annual meeting of the American Evaluation Association, Dallas, TX.

Rossi, P. H., Freeman, H. E., & Lipsey, M. W. (1999). *Evaluation: A systematic approach* (6th ed.). Thousand Oaks, CA: Sage.

Scriven, M. (1974). Evaluation perspectives and procedures. In W. J. Popham (Ed.), *Evaluation in education.* Berkeley, CA: McCutchan.

Scriven, M. (1991). *Evaluation thesaurus* (4th ed.). Newbury Park, CA: Sage.

Scriven, M. (1996). Types of evaluation and types of evaluators. *Evaluation Practice, 17,* 151-161.

Seefeldt, M. (1992, November). *Conflicts in conceptual framework, design, audience expectation, and evaluator style.* Paper presented at the annual meeting of the American Evaluation Association, Seattle, WA.

Smith, M. F. (1988). Evaluation utilization revisited. *New Directions for Program Evaluation, 39,* 7-20.

Smith, M. L., & Glass, G. V. (1987). *Research and evaluation in education and the social sciences.* Englewood Cliffs, NJ: Prentice Hall.

Stake, R. E. (1967). The countenance of educational evaluation. *Teachers College Record, 68,* 523-540.

Stake, R. E. (1978). The case study method in social inquiry. *Educational Researcher, 7,* 5-9.

Stake, R. E. (1983). Program evaluation, particularly responsive evaluation. In G. F. Madaus, M. Scriven, & D. L. Stufflebeam (Eds.), *Evaluation models* (pp. 287-310). Boston, MA: Kluwer-Nihoff.

Stevens, C. T., & Dial, M. (1994). What constitutes misuse? *New Directions for Program Evaluation, 64,* 3-14.

Stufflebeam, D. L. (1994). Empowerment evaluation, objectivist evaluation, and evaluation standards: Where the future of evaluation should not go and where it needs to go. *Evaluation Practice, 15,* 321-338.

Stufflebeam, D. L. (2000). The CIPP model of evaluation. In D. L. Stufflebeam, G. F. Madaus, & T. Kellaghan (Eds.), *Evaluation models: Viewpoints on educational and human services evaluation* (2nd ed., pp. 279-317). Boston, MA: Kluwer Academic.

Tests in print (5th ed.). (1999). Lincoln, NE: Buros Institute of Mental Measurements, University of Nebraska.

Tyler, R. W. (1949). *Basic principles of curriculum and instructions: Syllabus for Education 360.* Chicago, IL: University of Chicago Press.

Weiss, C. H. (1998). Have we learned anything new about the use of evaluation? *American Journal of Evaluation, 19,* 21-33.

Worthen, B. R., Sanders, J. R., & Fitzpatrick, J. L. (1997). *Educational evaluation: Alternative approaches and practical guidelines* (2nd ed.). New York: Addison Wesley Longman.

Yin, R. K. (1994). Evaluation: a singular craft. In C. S. Reichardt & S. F. Rallis (Eds.), The qualitative-quantitative debate: New perspectives. *New Directions for Program Evaluation, 61,* 71-84.

Index

About the Author

Rita G. O'Sullivan (Ed.D., 1984, Auburn University) is Associate Professor of Evaluation and Assessment at the University of North Carolina at Chapel Hill, where she teaches graduate courses in educational program evaluation, case study methods, research design, measurement, and statistics. She is also Executive Director of Evaluation, Assessment, and Policy Connections (EvAP), a unit she founded within the UNC School of Education that provides evaluation training for graduate students and professionals in addition to conducting local, state, national, and international evaluations. She has specialized in developing collaborative evaluation techniques that enhance evaluation capacity and utilization among educators and public service providers. She has successfully used collaborative evaluation approaches with education, health, community development, agriculture, and family support programs in North Carolina and with nonprofit organizations in the United States, as well as overseas. A sample of her evaluations includes the national evaluation of Project STAR and evaluations of the North Carolina Character Education Partnership; All Stars, Sr., a substance abuse prevention program for high school health education; distance education components of UNC-CH Masters in Education for Experienced Teachers; and the Childcare Initiative of First 5 for Los Angeles County. Among her publications is *Programs for At-Risk Students: A Guide to Evaluation* (Corwin Press, 1993). In 2001, she traveled to Siberia to conduct evaluation training for 160 staff from the emerging nonprofit sector in the newly independent states of the former USSR, and in 2003, she was invited to Brazil, where she conducted workshops on collaborative evaluation and delivered a keynote address at the second annual meeting of the Brazilian evaluation association. In addition to her contributions to the field of evaluation via articles and presentations, she served as Secretary/Treasurer of the American Evaluation Association from 1992 to 1997. In 2001, she was presented with the first lifetime Distinguished Service Award from the North Carolina Association for Research in Education, and in 2002, she received the Ingle Award for Service to the American Evaluation Association.